Computational Thinking and Coding for Every Student

To Jackson, James, my family, and the crew at Code.org: Thank you for your support and patience during the creation of this book.

—Kiki Prottsman

To my family and friends: Thank you for your encouragement and interest in this project!

—Jane Krauss

To all of the dedicated members of the CSEd community: Your hard work and dedication paved the way for a book like this. Thank you for your passion.

—The Authors

In memorium

In memory of Seymour Papert (1928–2016), the father of educational computing. As he suggested, may we all think of computers as mud pies—stuff to think with.

Praise for *Computational Thinking and Coding for Every Student*

Change in education and schooling comes in waves, and coding, computer science, and computational thinking represent the next very big wave. This very readable book will introduce teachers, parents, and students to the future.

—Dr. Neil MacNeill, PhD, EdD

This book will help a lot of educators take their first steps toward bringing high quality programming experiences to their students. It offers clear examples and good strategies supported by research and best practices.

—Sylvia Martinez, Co-author of *Invent To Learn: Making, Tinkering, and Engineering in the Classroom*, www.InventToLearn.com

Wondering whether this book is for you? Check out the "dos and don'ts" of Chapter 5 and then take them to heart. I did!

—Dr. James Cohoon, Department of Computer Science, University of Virginia

This book is so clear and so encouraging. I recommend it to my Girls Excelling in Math and Science (GEMS) leaders as we work to incorporate more computer science into our activities. The authors present a comprehensive introduction to computing in a way that's useful, readable, and fun.

—Laura Reasoner Jones

Computational Thinking and Coding for Every Student

The Teacher's Getting-Started Guide

Jane Krauss

Kiki Prottsman

Foreword by Pat Yongpradit of Code.org

CORWIN

A SAGE Publishing Company

FOR INFORMATION:

Corwin

A SAGE Company

2455 Teller Road

Thousand Oaks, California 91320

www.corwin.com

SAGE Ltd.

1 Oliver's Yard

55 City Road

London EC1Y 1SP

United Kingdom

SAGE Pvt. Ltd.

B 1/I 1 Mohan Cooperative Industrial Area

Mathura Road, New Delhi 110 044

India

SAGE Publications Asia-Pacific Pte. Ltd.

3 Church Street

#10–04 Samsung Hub

Singapore 049483

Acquisitions Editor: Erin Null

Developmental Editor: Julie Nemer

Editorial Assistant: Nicole Shade

Production Editor: Veronica Stapleton Hooper

Copy Editor: Colleen Brennan

Typesetter: C&M Digitals (P) Ltd.

Proofreader: Jeff Bryant

Indexer: Marilyn Augst

Cover Designer: Scott Van Atta

Marketing Manager: Rebecca Eaton

Names: Krauss, Jane, author. | Prottsman, Kiki, author.

Title: Computational thinking and coding for every student : the teacher's getting-started guide / Jane Krauss, Kiki Prottsman; Foreword by Pat Yongpradit of Code.org

Description: Thousand Oaks, California : Corwin, 2016. | Includes bibliographical references and index.

Identifiers: LCCN 2016031158 | ISBN 9781506341286 (pbk. : alk. paper)

Subjects: LCSH: Computer science—Study and teaching (Elementary) | Computer science—Study and teaching (Secondary) | Computer programming—Study and teaching (Elementary) | Computer programming—Study and teaching (Secondary) | Computational learning theory.

Classification: LCC QA76.27 .K73 2016 | DDC 004.071—dc23

LC record available at https://lccn.loc.gov/2016031158

This book is printed on acid-free paper.

20 10 9 8 7 6 5

Contents

Note from the Publisher: The authors have provided video and web content throughout the book which is available to you through QR Codes. To read a QR Code, you must have a smartphone or tablet with a camera. We recommend that you download a QR Code reader app that is made specifically for your phone or tablet brand.

 Additional resources are available at resources.corwin.com/Computational Thinking

Foreword

Dear reader,

Don't do what I did (or what most teachers do).

I transitioned from teaching science to teaching computer science at a time when teachers were still using plastic transparencies for overhead projectors. There weren't books on how to teach computer science, let alone computational thinking. So I read books meant for professional software engineers. I did internet searches for "computer science lessons" and found links to university professors' presentation slides. I scraped together whatever I could find and then ended up spending hours creating my own activities and lesson plans. You are probably teaching multiple subjects. You probably don't have a background in computer science. Maybe you are a parent who is just trying to give your kids an opportunity that they are not receiving in school. So unless you like reinventing the wheel and have gobs of available time, don't do what I did.

Read this book.

As chief academic officer at Code.org, a national non-profit organization that promotes computer science education, I wake up every day wondering how teachers are faring in a climate in which everyone and their mother (and even principals) are jumping on the "coding" bandwagon. I know people are being "voluntold" to teach computer science. I know that district specialists are being asked to install computer science programs. I know that parents are asking schools, "Do we teach coding?" I worry that even teachers with the best intentions don't know where to start.

Read this book.

Kiki Prottsman and Jane Krauss are exactly the people I'd want writing a book for people interested in computer science education. These two have been at the forefront of the rising popularity of computer science and are experts in the issues that the field faces, such as equity and diversity. In this book, they've condensed years of research and practitioner experience into an easy-to-read narrative about what computer science is, why it is important, and how to teach it to a variety of audiences. Their ideas aren't just good, they are research-based and have been in practice in thousands of classrooms. How do I know? As a teacher I used the National Center for Women in Technology's resources to understand the issues women and underrepresented minorities face in computer science and learn how to advocate for greater diversity, as well as opportunities in computer science. At Code.org, I've recommended Jane's "Programs-in-a-Box" and incorporated her Counselors for Computing program into the professional development we offer to administrators and counselors in the districts we serve. As for Kiki, well she was the driving force behind the look, feel, and content of our CS Fundamentals program, a curriculum that has reached millions of kids worldwide and a professional development program that has trained tens of thousands of teachers through a nationwide network of more than two hundred facilitators. Kiki believes that computer science is fun, and she's infused that ethic into each chapter of this book. She's crafted tutorials, designed her own coding magazine, and she has purple hair–what more could you ask for?

While not a comprehensive list, in this book you'll find:

- Current, vetted resources—both printable and online

- Real lesson ideas. Not the ones that take hours to read, require equipment you don't have, and promise 45 minutes, but take 90 minutes— but the ones that are easy to teach and will keep kids engaged and excited.

- Simple explanations of hard computer science ideas with real-world examples and connections to other disciplines.

- Something for everyone. Formal and informal educators. In-school and out-of-school. Elementary, middle, and high school.

So to the hundreds and thousands of teachers who are considering, learning, or actively teaching computer science—this book is well worth your time.

Read this book.

Thank you for doing what you do to support computer science education,

Pat Yongpradit
Chief Academic Officer, Code.org

Preface

Computational Thinking and Coding for Every Student is a book about teaching computer science, but in practice, it's so much more. This book is about curiosity, problem solving, and testing your own boundaries as a learner and as an educator. It's about making, dreaming, innovating, and encouraging the same in your students.

Computational Thinking and Coding for Every Student is for the K–12 educator who has little to no experience in computer science. Our aim is to help you understand what computing is, why it's important, and how computing fits into your larger curriculum. You will have many opportunities to try computer science yourself and see firsthand how computing activities not only teach computer science but support critical thinking more generally.

Although you won't find a full curriculum for computer science for every grade in this book, you will encounter a plentiful assortment of exercises and lesson plans. These are meant to provide exposure to key concepts as well as inspiration for where you and your students might go next. After sampling the exercises and testing out the lessons, don't be surprised if you start imagining ways to incorporate computing into the subjects you teach. When you're ready for more, hop over to our companion site at resources.corwin.com/ComputationalThinking and follow the links to more advanced content.

Until recently, computer science was largely an unknown entity in K–12 education. In the pages that follow, we encourage you to think of computer science as inquiry and as art. The programming industry is full of creative and functional storytellers; as a matter of fact, our development process closely mimics that of filmmaking. From storyboarding to production, we will show you how computer science is the movie set where all of your students can become stars!

WHY THIS BOOK? WHY NOW?

Roughly 90 percent of U.S. parents believe that offering computer science would be a good use of school resources and more than 65 percent think computer science should be required in school (Google, 2015). Teachers, principals, and superintendents increasingly recognize computer science as a "go to" skill set, but, on the face of it, taking the first steps toward providing computer science can seem daunting. As educators, we can picture what it takes to teach other science, technology, engineering, and math (STEM) subjects; we all have personal experience with them as learners, and some of us as teachers, and we're all consumers of science news. Computer science can feel less approachable because it's unfamiliar and, on the surface (all that code!), may seem complicated.

We wrote this book to change the perception and reputation of computer science (CS). Teaching and learning CS doesn't have to be daunting or tedious. It's an ever-changing craft that encourages students to think for themselves, analyze problems, and try new approaches regularly. As an educator, you don't have to be an expert to teach computer science. We recommend that teachers learn right alongside their students, and we present this book to fortify you for the journey ahead.

As we go to print, only a quarter of high schools teach computer science in high school, with even fewer teaching it in the lower grades (Google, 2015). In early 2016, only thirty-two states count computer science coursework toward graduation, usually as science or math credit (Code.org, 2016). For the rest, when CS is offered it counts as an elective, which means many of our busiest students can't take it. Because of these barriers, only families of means are likely to seek extracurricular opportunities for their children to develop the critical computer science skills relevant to the emerging job market. Almost everyone else will graduate without them.

Fortunately, change is afoot. In January 2016, the White House announced "Computer Science for All," an initiative that aims to "empower a generation of American students with the computer science skills they need to thrive in a digital economy" (Smith, 2016). This ambitious call to action positions computer science as a basic literacy, a necessary skill set for any student joining the workforce of the future. There is no time left to postpone the introduction of computer science in K–12 schools. Parents are ready. Students are ready. With "Computer Science for All," state departments of education and school districts are getting ready, too.

Momentum for CS can be attributed to efforts by many nonprofit organizations, community groups, government agencies, universities, and private corporations. More than *100 million* children worldwide have tried their hand at computing through Code.org's Hour of Code and are ready for more.

Makerspaces and CoderDojos (open source and volunteer-led coding clubs for young people) are springing up in communities large and small across the nation. The National Science Foundation and other organizations are funding professional development to prepare more than 35,000 educators to teach computer science in the next five years. Google's CS4HS and Microsoft's TEALS programs are enhancing computer science teaching around the country. The National Center for Women & Information Technology consults with all of these groups, advising on practices to make computer science accessible to girls and women.

Some of the country's largest school districts consider computer science "the new normal". Los Angeles Unified, Miami-Dade, Chicago, and New York City school districts are establishing new curricula, with the last three districts projecting that every child will learn CS every year. On the state level, Arkansas recently passed the first truly comprehensive legislation that commits all public and charter schools to teach computer science.

Students have more education choices than ever, including free courses from Code.org, CodeHS, and Khan Academy. The Massachusetts Institute of Technology (MIT), Harvard University, and Stanford University have even packaged their introductory computer science courses into free, online offerings for older students . . . or maybe even you!

WHAT TO EXPECT

In our early chapters, we introduce you to the concepts of computer science and computational thinking. With a quick dip into decomposition, pattern matching, abstraction, and algorithms, you'll see how core elements of computer science are reflected in activities we engage in every day. You'll experience computational thinking as a set of problem-solving techniques that are useful in many areas of our lives.

Before getting into the fundamentals of coding, we take the opportunity in Chapter 1 to correct some misunderstandings about what computer science is and is not. We clear up confusion about the differences between learning to use computers and learning computer science, and we set the record straight about who is right for computing.

In Chapter 2 you will see why computing is a fundamental literacy all students should have the opportunity to develop. Because computer science underpins modern innovation and business today, those equipped with computing skills can pursue a wide array of interests and enjoy rewarding careers. And, because this core set of skills is applicable to any type of inquiry or investigation, all students stand to benefit, no matter what they ultimately want to "be" when they grow up. Then, looking beyond what CS learning does for the individual, we also consider why the world needs more—and more kinds of—people contributing to the research, products, and services based in computer science.

Next, we challenge you to dive in. With an emphasis on pair programming (a method for partnering for better code), Chapter 3 leads you directly into the world of computing. You will experience the satisfaction of working through problems and puzzles as you "think aloud" with a friend or colleague.

The pressures and problems of the classroom are certainly not lost on us, and in Chapter 4 we address issues around screen time, technology access, the crowded curriculum, digital citizenship, and program costs.

Chapter 5 is a summary of dos and don'ts, useful advice for getting started with CS. Then, in Chapter 6, we return to computational thinking for a deeper dive, and in Chapters 7 through 10, we address the "pillars" of computational thinking and provide learning activities that develop each.

Spatial reasoning is another aspect of cognition central to computing, and in Chapter 11 we consider how spatial skills help us move from the concrete to the abstract and back again as we program computers. This chapter ends with tips for "spatializing" your teaching, and is followed by Chapter 12, which delves into the *very* spatial hands-on and minds-on maker movement that is taking schools by storm.

In Chapters 13 through 17 we consider a scenario for a complete K–12 pathway, with advice, resources, and lessons for in-school time, and suggestions for informal learning in the after-school setting, too. Chapter 18 focuses on creating and adapting lessons for your students. Finally, we wrap up with Chapter 19, stories from the field and testimonials from inspired (and inspiring) teachers.

You can amplify your reading experience by dipping into the companion website as you go. What you'll find there are links to all the browser-based learning activities we describe in the book, expanded content relating to the topics we address, and useful resources and stories from schools not so different from yours.

A NOTE ABOUT PREPARATION

We recommend you keep a laptop or digital tablet with you as you read. In addition to using it to capture your questions or notes for discussion, you'll want to browse digital content as you go.

Throughout this book you will find web-based resources to examine and coding activities to try. So you don't have to type out cumbersome URLs (web addresses), we supply QR codes for you to scan. QR, or "quick response" codes, are readable from smartphones and tablets with cameras. A quick scan will take you to the website we've recommended, right at the perfect point in the reading.

In order to scan QR codes, you need an app. Many free QR scanner apps are available. RedLaser and Scan are two app providers you might check out. Just search these names or "QR code reader" to find one that works for you. Go ahead and try this right now. We'll wait!

After you're done, try your first scan using the QR code shown here. It will take you to the Facebook page for this book. (If you want to get to the companion site the old-fashioned way, it's located at facebook.com/groups/ CodingInClass.)

One more note: Throughout the book and starting in Chapter 2, you will see asterisks (*) associated with resources that are worth your while. All of these are included on the companion site with a short description and web link that leads you to more information.

LIGHTS, CAMERA, ACTION!

Computer science is about to hit the big screen and we want you at the premiere! Recruit a friend or two to join you, then kick things off with Chapter 1. Don't forget to keep track of your questions and comments along the way so you can share them with fellow readers and on social media.

Acknowledgments

This book represents a timely partnership between education, organization, and a visionary group of publishers. As authors, we would like to extend our heartfelt appreciation to the team at Corwin for actively working to make this book a reality.

PUBLISHER'S ACKNOWLEDGMENTS

Corwin gratefully acknowledges the contributions of the following reviewers:

April K. DeGennaro
Teacher, Gifted Resource
Fayette County Board of Education
Fayetteville, Georgia

Sarah Filman
VP of Curriculum
Code.org
Seattle, Washington

Becky Wilson Hawbaker
Field Experience Coordinator
University of Northern Iowa
Cedar Falls, Iowa

Patti Hendricks
Language Arts Teacher
Sunset Ridge Middle School
West Jordan, Utah

Christine Landwehrle
Assistant Director of Curriculum and Professional Development
Amherst, Mont Vernon and Souhegan Cooperative School Districts
Amherst, New Hampshire

Alexis Ludewig
Supervisor of Student Teachers
University of Wisconsin, Oshkosh
Oshkosh, Wisconsin

Neil MacNeill
Head Master
Ellenbrook Independent Primary School
Ellenbrook, Western Australia

Toni B. Ramey
Middle School Science Teacher
Mobile County Public School System
Mobile, Alabama

Karen Shade
Lecturer, Computing, Software and Data Sciences
California Baptist University
Riverside, California

About the Authors

Jane Krauss is coauthor with Suzie Boss of the bestselling book *Reinventing Project-Based Learning*. A longtime teacher and technology enthusiast, Jane is currently a curriculum and program development consultant to organizations interested in project-based approaches to teaching and learning. Among others, she works with the National Center for Women & Information Technology, paving the way for inclusive practices that encourage the meaningful participation of girls and women in computing. In addition, Jane teaches online courses in project-based learning, speaks at conferences, and presents professional development workshops in the United States and internationally. In her free time Jane enjoys dabbling in glasswork and mosaics, and keeps fit running and hiking on woodland trails just outside her door in Eugene, Oregon.

Kiki Prottsman is Education Program Manager at Code.org and a former computer science instructor at the University of Oregon. As a member of Mensa and a past chair of Women in Computer Science, she also writes for the *Huffington Post* and has graced the cover of *Open for Business* magazine.

As a champion for responsible computing and equity in both computer science employment and education, Kiki works with organizations to improve the experience of girls and women in the fields of science, technology, engineering, and math. Her landmark work with the hands-on Traveling Circuits computer science curriculum helped Thinkersmith receive the 2013 Google RISE Award for excellence in science and engineering. She currently sits on the Advisory Board for Wonder Workshop Robotics and is a vital member of the leadership team for the Oregon Girls Collaborative Project.

Part 1
Storyboarding

The computing fields are full of creative and functional storytellers. As you read, notice parallels we've drawn with an industry you might be familiar with—filmmaking. From storyboarding to production, we will show you how computer science is the movie set where all of your students become stars!

In the next few chapters, see the "big picture" of what computer science is and who it's for (everybody), and start imagining the outline of your script for bringing computer science to school.

1

An Introduction to Computer Science

COMPUTER SCIENCE IS WITHIN YOU

Have you ever completed a Sudoku puzzle? Can you sing or play a tune from sheet music? Can you decipher a knitting pattern or follow steps to fold an origami figure? If you've ever attempted any of these things, then you have already experienced one of the fundamental building blocks in computer science (CS), the **algorithm**.

The word *algorithm* may sound technical and scary, but really it's just a list of steps that can be followed to carry out a task. We see algorithms every day when we engage in activities that have instructions. Games, recipes, and crafts all become physical representations of algorithms, unknowingly aligning us with our family computers—because in the end, algorithms are also at the heart of every piece of code.

Algorithm: A list of steps that can be followed to carry out a task.

In this book, we'll encourage you to explore your relationship with that digital diva, the personal computer. We'll act as guides, taking you from familiar territory into new terrain, where you'll interact with computers as a medium for invention. Start imagining how you'll equip your students for this journey, following President Obama's advice:

> **“**Don't just buy a new video game, make one. Don't just download the latest app, help design it. Don't just play on your phone, program it! **”**
>
> —President Barack Obama (quoted in Machaber, 2014)

As you prepare to dive into computing activities in the pages to come, pack up your enthusiasm for learning new things, arm yourself with a growth mindset, and start imagining limitless possibilities!

By the way, here's the first line of code ever written by a U.S. president:

    moveForward(100);

If Obama can do it, you and your students can too!

Now, let's kick things off by investigating the underpinnings of CS—computational thinking. A brief scan here will ground you in the concept. We provide a more comprehensive look in Chapters 6 through 10 (with lesson plans!).

AN INTRODUCTION TO COMPUTATIONAL THINKING

The buzz around **computational thinking** began in the early 2000s when Jeannette M. Wing, a professor of computer science at Carnegie Mellon University, introduced the term in a series of academic papers (Wing, 2006). At the time, she presented computational thinking as a set of attitudes and skills a person would need to confidently persist toward identifying, posing, and solving problems. The term soon morphed to include capabilities that apply to preparation for CS. We'll explore these critical capabilities, as well as pay respect to the original concept of open-minded problem solving that sometimes goes missing in today's world of standardized testing and scripted lessons.

> **Computational thinking**: Using special thinking patterns and processes to pose and solve problems or prepare programs for computation. Notably decomposition, pattern matching, abstraction, and automation.

Distilled down to its most fundamental elements, computational thinking is comprised of four pillars:

- Decomposition
- Pattern matching
- Abstraction, and
- Algorithms (sometimes referred to as *automation*)

With these four skills, one can prepare any problem for a mechanical solution. But what does that really mean? Let's unpack each element as we consider something you're likely familiar with, a sudoku puzzle (Figure 1.1).

These little grids seem unassuming enough, but once you start to play, you'll see they're packed with complexity. The point of a sudoku is to fill in all the blank squares with digits (typically 1 through 9) in such a way that there is exactly one of each digit in any given column, row, or block of cells.

Even with a ton of experience solving these little enigmas, it can still be quite challenging to describe how to go about it. If we want to prepare a sudoku *algorithm* (a procedure or formula) for *automation* (running on a machine), we're going to need to use some computational thinking.

7	8	1	2	4	6	9		
	3	9			1	4	7	
4	5	2			9	8	6	
	9	5		2			1	8
2			7	1		5	3	9
1	7		5			2		6
	2	3	4	6	7	1		5
8	1				5		2	7
	6			8	2	3		

FIGURE 1.1   Standard 9 × 9 Sudoku

First, let's use **decomposition** on the problem by con-sciously identifying the list of steps we might go through to figure out what should happen in each space. For ease of explanation, let's focus on one 4 × 4 square at a time in the mini-puzzle below, beginning with the upper left blank cell (row 1, column 1).

Decomposition: Breaking a problem down into smaller, more manageable parts.

Figure 1.2 below is a simple version of a sudoku puzzle. How would you determine what goes into the first empty corner? As a human, I might fol-low an algorithm like this:

1. Look at the numbers that are missing in row 1. (That would be 1 and 2.)

2. Look at the numbers that are missing in column 1. (That would be 2 and 3.)

3. Look at the numbers missing in quad-rant 1. (That would be 1 and 2.)

4. If there is only one number missing from all three sets, that is the number that goes in the upper left cell. (And that would be 2!)

5. If there is a second number missing from all three sets, continue to the next cell and come back when you have more information.

	3	4	
4			2
1			3
	2	1	

FIGURE 1.2   Simplified 4 × 4 Sudoku

Sure, we've made this a bit straightforward, but the strategy should hold when it comes to solving for any individual cell. Now, to illustrate, let's look at the steps for the cell in row 2, column 3. (No answers this time!)

1. Look at the numbers that are missing in row 2.

2. Look at the numbers that are missing in column 3.

3. Look at the numbers missing in quadrant 2.

4. If there is only one number missing from all three sets, that is the number that goes in the square.

5. If there is a second number missing from all three sets, continue to the next square and come back when you have more information.

At this point, we can apply more computational thinking to try to get an algorithm that will work for automating the discovery of a solution for any sudoku.

Pattern matching: Finding similarities between items as a way of gaining extra information.

Here, we will use **pattern matching**. Do you see any patterns between our first set of steps and our second? Let's compare the first instruction in both.

Look at the numbers that are missing in row 1.

Look at the numbers that are missing in row 2.

The instructions are nearly identical. As a matter of fact, if you were to list out steps for each and every cell, you would find that the only thing that changed was the number of the row that you were working with. That's a pattern! What can we do with it?

Abstraction: Ignoring certain details in order to come up with a solution that works for a more general problem.

This is where **abstraction** comes in. Abstraction is simply the act of removing details that are too specific, so that one instruction can work for multiple problems.

To complete the abstraction on the instructions above, we might turn the sentence into something like this:

Look at the numbers that are missing in row _____.

The blank now becomes a spot where you enter the row number of the empty square that you are currently working with.

Can you take the rest of the instructions and abstract them out so that you wind up with a final algorithm for automation of a sudoku of this size? Did you come up with a different method altogether?

Mental Agility

How do you feel while working at puzzles like sudoku, deciphering crochet patterns, learning new sheet music, or following diagrams to put together Ikea furniture? Do you feel the burn as you stretch your mental muscles? Do you enter a state of "flow" when deeply immersed? Do you find yourself surprised at how time flies when you're so engaged that every other concern seems to vanish? Are you deeply satisfied when troubleshooting helps you overcome obstacles and move forward? At the very least, aren't you pleased to have applied cognitive effort to a new challenge?

The kind of mental workout we've been talking about is similar to what one might feel as a genuine, bona fide, creative problem solver taking the first steps toward becoming a computer scientist. Get ready for more opportunities to apply your computational thinking to exercises and web activities in the next chapters, and prepare for a deeper dive into computational thinking in Chapters 6 through 10.

WHAT COMPUTER SCIENCE IS

You can think of **computer science** as the study of how to use computers and computational thinking to solve problems, not merely the act of using technology. It's like the difference between watching a movie and producing and directing one (Figure 1.3). We already have a generation of filmgoers; now we need more producers and directors (software designers, developers, and programmers) who can create the vast array of products and services the world needs.

> **Computer science**: The study and use of computers and computational thinking to solve problems.

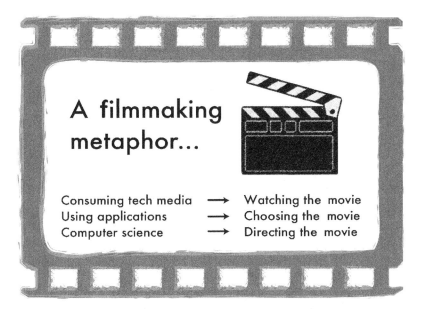

FIGURE 1.3 A Filmmaking Metaphor

In the Beginning

You may be surprised to find out that CS as we know it developed a full thirty years before the first reprogrammable computer (Rabin, 2012). It all came about when Alan Turing and Alonzo Church theorized that there were definite limits on what could be computed using methods of **automation**, formalizing the idea of algorithms in the process.

Automation: Controlling a process by automatic means, reducing human intervention to a minimum.

Since then, CS has evolved from the study of what can be automated to the practice of automating with finesse! Computer science and computational thinking are not the same thing, but computational thinking is a vital component when it comes to translating real-world situations or solutions into algorithms. In this book, we will often mention one without the other, but we do so with the understanding that the two are strongest together.

WHAT COMPUTER SCIENCE IS NOT

Next, and almost equally as important as knowing what computer science *is*, is knowing what computer science *is not*. Often, families and educators believe their students are learning CS because they are in a class that meets in the computer lab several times a week. More often than not, these sessions deal with learning to use specific software, such as a word processor or graphic design program. These are great reasons to work with computers, but they aren't CS.

Computer science is an excellent tool for developing students' digital skills. In the process of learning CS, even the youngest kids learn to use a keyboard, copy and paste, save files, and access the internet effectively and responsibly. CS encompasses these frequently taught skills, but the converse isn't true.

Let's address some other aspects of what CS *is not*. CS is not boring. It is not a solitary act, and it is not an advanced subject that's practiced only by the most brilliant or privileged. CS is a set of beautiful, digital art forms that allow you to express your thoughts and feelings while you innovate and provide solutions for humanity. CS is a growing subject, full of unexplored potential and room for deviation. It is not static or depleted.

CS is also not *just* programming. While you might be hard-pressed to describe the difference between the two terms, give us a few paragraphs and you won't be anymore.

Programming is just one specific area of CS. It is most often thought of as writing code for a machine, but programming also encompasses the thought processes, design structures, and **debugging** that occur while coding. Talking about the programming process of CS is a lot like talking about the scriptwriting process. It is a supremely important element that provides the road map for the finished product, but there are many other pieces to consider. In filmmaking, those pieces might include acting, directing, and editing; in CS, they include software engineering, user interfaces, and hardware design.

Debugging: To track down and correct errors.

People are also confused about the difference between *programming* and *coding*. This distinction is a little more nuanced. For the most part, the two terms can be used interchangeably, but to people who care, there is a difference.

It used to be that just about everyone who wrote code was a *programmer*. They were educated specialists who took pride in their craft and put great thought into the programs they wrote. In the 1980s and 1990s, more and more people began to teach themselves to develop computer code. The details of logical and beautiful design were not always embedded into the work of this new generation of self-made technologists, often referred to as *hackers* or *coders* by their professional counterparts.

Today, the term *hacker* has taken on a more sinister connotation, whereas the label *coder* continues to describe someone who can piece together a program but may not have the chops to design code with finesse. As such, a professional programmer may not take kindly to being called a *coder*.

That said, we frequently use the term *coding* in this book because it is appropriate when describing programming at an entry level. We will also frequently refer to *programming* and *computer science* when talking about practices, classes, or curricula that encompass more than an introductory glimpse of code.

As you read the rest of this book, we will show you not only how you can test the CS waters on your own but also how you can bring this capability to your students, beginning even with prereaders. No matter what your level of experience, this is a journey worth taking. So, if you're still concerned about this digital trek . . . don't worry, we've got you!

2

Why Kids Should Have the Opportunity to Learn

Like a good film, the world of coding can draw children into the screen, allowing them to experience new worlds. For better or for worse, it can also be a distraction from the actual world they live in. There is an enthusiastic roar for "unplugging" and withdrawing from the digital domain to gather peace and to center ourselves. The importance of exposing young kids to computer science (CS) has been questioned and, in some cases, discouraged. All the conflict, however, tends to focus on time engaged with technology as a tool rather than the craft itself.

In its earliest stages, CS doesn't require a computer any more than mathematics requires a scientific calculator. The need for technology doesn't arise as a requirement until a strong foundation is built, yet parents, educators, and school administrators still express concern when the topic of introducing CS comes up.

The question must be asked, is it better to teach our children responsible computing during their critical period of mental development, or pass up the benefit of an absorbent mind in favor of more traditional, non-digital tasks?

Let's explore this question with a thought exercise.

Imagine you wake up one day in a country where students don't learn mathematics. There are no elementary school math tests, and numbers are merely quantities rather than majestic players in grand equations.

In this country, students don't know math in middle school. They begin to hear about formulas in high school, but very few classrooms actually teach them. In fact, students might get all the way to their senior year in college before they actually decide to take a class on mathematics, and even then it would be an elective that they only chose because their uncle on their mother's side said they might be able to make a lot of money someday, since many of the jobs in the future will require math.

Now imagine that students, finally deciding to explore this subject, enter the classroom to find that they need to master the whole of numeracy, arithmetic, algebra, geometry, and trigonometry in their very first term. What chance do they have of developing a passion for the field? What chance do these students have of feeling that they were prepared for the experience?

Obviously, this story is meant to draw an analogy to CS in the United States. Ten years ago, this may not have felt like a fitting parallel, but with more and more countries bringing CS into the classroom and teaching young students the fundamentals of CS, the rest of us risk trailing behind educationally.

WHAT COMPUTER SCIENCE REALLY TEACHES

When this book's coauthor Kiki Prottsman launched Thinkersmith and started developing CS lessons for kindergartners, it wasn't to create a secret army of miniature programmers. Instead, her goal was to show young people that CS is a creative means of self-expression. She often compares programming to refrigerator magnet haiku that emotes a great deal of meaning, even under a narrow set of predefined rules.

When you learn how to think creatively in a restrictive environment, barriers become provocative challenges rather than boundaries, and the landscape of a problem changes from desolate and impossible to a field of hidden opportunities.

During her time working with students in elementary school, one of the biggest heartaches Kiki encountered was the lack of confidence students have in their own thought processes. When a child hears that there is a challenge that no one has ever solved, their common reaction is self-doubt. The real magic of CS is the ability to consistently present problems that have never been solved and allow students the experience of being the very first to do so, in their own unique way. When students learn that they can effect change, they look at the world with an entirely different view. When students learn that each failure is a clue for what to try next, they stop thinking of failing as a frustration and begin to look at it as an element of exploration. Think of all that a person could accomplish if "I can't" were to be replaced with "I'll figure out a way!"

> **"**I don't think everyone will be a coder, but the ability to speak and structure your thinking in a way a computer understands it will be one of the core future skills whatever your field.**"**
>
> —Linda Liukas, founder,
> *Rails Girls Coding Community*

That's what CS teaches. It's a medium for solving problems, complete with a tool for instant feedback and the opportunity for practicing persistence toward a goal.

When a student learns that each failure is a clue for what to try next, they stop thinking of failing as a frustration and begin to look at it as an element of exploration.

In the world of CS education, some distinguishing elements include:

- Creativity
- Collaboration
- Communication
- Persistence
- Problem Posing and Problem Solving

Here is a brief explanation of each element and some examples of the role that CS plays in their development:

Creativity—This is a beautiful word. Evoking the image of a wild-eyed inventor, we associate creativity with innovation and passion. CS is an incubator for creativity in every form, inspiring students to come up with new ways of looking at old situations, and encouraging them to use classic techniques on new problems. With the instant gratification of a fast-running program, students can ask "What if . . ." and check their craziest ideas immediately.

Collaboration—We all know that computer scientists do all of their work alone in the cold, dark basement, right? No, isolated lairs are only meant for mad scientists and superheroes, not productive teams of programmers. Many well-known tech companies, like Google and Facebook, have moved to large, bright, community workspaces to encourage collaboration. Some companies, such as Twitter, Groupon, and Pivotal Labs, even encourage **pair programming** so that one person is looking for solutions and pitfalls as the other writes code. The best technology comes from a series of diverse viewpoints. This goal is achieved via the combination of many minds, many eyes, and many mouths! We will talk more about pair programming later in this book.

Pair programming: An agile software development technique in which two programmers work together at one computer. The "driver" writes code while the "navigator" reviews and advises on code as it is typed. The two programmers switch roles frequently.

Communication—As with filmmaking, truly epic titles cannot be released without several teams of people lending their expertise to the project.

These teams need to be able to communicate with each other effectively and often.

The general public used to think of programmers and software engineers as solitary and antisocial, but this is not the case. When working in a CS field, team members need to be able to express their ideas, understand the requirements being presented to them, and estimate how much work it will take to complete a job. Often, this process requires a significant amount of back-and-forth with their team and their clients.

Persistence—Never give up! Seriously, don't do it. CS is a game in which the biggest rule is "Learn from failure." Many of you follow the work of Angela Duckworth, who advises that we help students develop "grit," and Carol Dweck, whose psychology research shows a **growth mindset** develops through persistence in the face of obstacles. Both scholars advise educators to intervene when students struggle, but in minimal, strategic, and supporting ways. (Stigler and Hiebert's [2009] longitudinal research into math instruction worldwide shows U.S. teachers are more likely to demonstrate the path to a right answer than are Japanese teachers, who encourage students to vary their attempts at problem solving.) Interestingly enough, in programming, failures aren't always mistakes! Often, we will send ourselves hurling into failures on purpose so we can examine the result and figure out what the error is telling us. These "fail" cases are data points to add to our growing collection of ideas. Soon, the data will illustrate a pattern, and that pattern will lead us right to the answer that we have been looking for. I've heard many teachers say "FAIL = First Attempt in Learning" (Figure 2.1), but failure is just as powerful when it's the fifth, fifteenth, or five-thousandth attempt . . . so keep on trying!

> **Growth mindset**: The personal belief that one's intelligence is not innate and fixed but develops through effort.

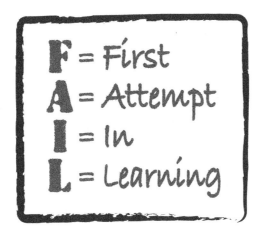

FIGURE 2.1 Encourage students to redefine what it means to F.A.I.L.!

Problem Posing and Problem Solving—When students master approaches to problem solving, they master life. There is strength in learning not to be thrown by every curve ball and hurdle. CS is full of opportunities to identify and solve problems and sharpen problem-solving techniques. One computing example, systematic inquiry, is a skill used when debugging in order to narrow the source of an issue and highlight a solution. Another is analyzing options—something you do when playing with **if statements**—in order to see there are multiple ways around a hurdle.

Certainly there are other facets to consider, but problem solving is integral to CS. If you scan the education standards for the subjects you teach, you will find *problem solving* called out in many of them. Domains as distinct as business education and music present problem solving as a key capability, and because most CS activities are situated in a subject matter context, they do double duty in building students' problem-solving muscles, no matter what they are studying.

A LOOK BACK

Before computers came equipped with a graphical user interface, applications software, and the ability to connect with remote devices, a computer did only what its user programmed it to do. If the user wanted the computer to calculate sums, he or she would write a computer program (i.e., lines of code) that would direct the computer to receive inputs (such as numbers), carry out a function (e.g., addition), and produce an output (a sum, for instance). Today much of the activity in computers is hidden from the user, and most programs are written by experts with special training.

Back when a computer user was, by necessity, a computer programmer, CS education had some serious traction. We can almost reach back to the roots of modern progressive education through those who first brought computer programming to school. In the early 1970s MIT computer scientist, mathematician, and educator Seymour Papert, a protégé of early childhood theorist Jean Piaget, brought CS into the classroom. He introduced children to CS through Logo, an educational programming language that operated on the most basic of computers. If a child programmer wanted a computer to draw, she would write a computer program in Logo for this purpose—no off-the-shelf software, no web-based drawing program, and certainly no Adobe Illustrator to take the work out of her hands. Presented with a very simple interface, the child wrote commands directly to the computer's console, which caused a "turtle" (a robot cursor of sorts) to draw on the screen.

A sample of Logo code and the snowflake the program rendered is shown in Figure 2.2.

papert—logo in your browser

examples: <u>koch snowflake</u>, <u>hilbert curve</u>, <u>spiral</u>

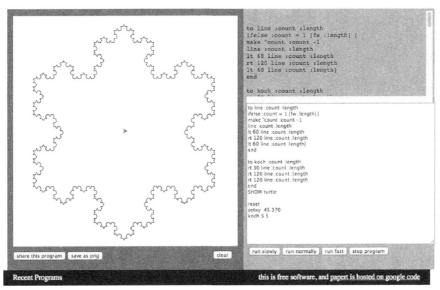

FIGURE 2.2 This modern version of Logo, fittingly called "Papert," operates in most any web browser.

Copyright © 2016 Papert

If you have tried your hand at coding, you may have a sense of what Papert meant when he compared computers to mud pies, both being "stuff to think with" (Papert, 1980). CS is a medium to express ideas. The action that results when you set the program you've written to "run" will always be no more and no less than what you transmitted through code. Think about all the problems solved and creative media that are brought to life through programming.

Papert is credited with expanding the conversation about progressive education from *constructivism* (constructing meaning through inquiry) to *constructionism,* which posits that learning happens best through building things that are tangible and shareable (Ackermann, Gauntlett, Wolbers, & Weckstrom, 2010). The philosophy behind the growing Maker movement in education (see more in Chapter 11) rests on the logic of constructionism.

Instead of thinking of the computer as a device that merely hosts applications and syncs to other devices, think of a computer as a raw material—a "mud pie" medium—limited only by the creativity of its user. Shifting your thinking this way will help you be a better facilitator of learning. You will be less likely to say "Kids, here's what we're doing today, now follow steps a, b, and c," and more likely to ask, "What are you trying to accomplish? Where are you in the work so far?"

Because of this, your students will be empowered. They are more likely to trust themselves to try something new. This is how innovation begins.

> *The computer is incredibly fast, accurate and stupid. Man is incredibly slow, inaccurate and brilliant. The marriage of the two is a force beyond calculation.*
>
> —Leo Cherne, economist and leader of international relief

Where might students' inventiveness lead? Some kids want to invent the next blockbuster video game, but many want to change the world we live in. Here is a glimpse of what kids can do when presented with a challenge to do just that.

- An eight-year-old in Connecticut uses Scratch to program her MaKey MaKey,* a printed circuit board with a microcontroller, to control a cat treat dispenser she built with Lego blocks.

Notice that MaKey MaKey is marked with an asterisk? Any resource worthy of your attention is marked this way and is listed with a corresponding link on the companion website for this book. Please see resources.corwin.com/ ComputationalThinking.

- A Delaware fourth grader uses a three-dimensional (3D) printer and design software to fabricate his own new prosthetic hand.

Winners of the 2015 Verizon Innovation App Challenge (Oddy, 2015) came up with history-making ideas, and then MIT helped them with app development:

- Kyrene Aprende Middle School students in Chandler, Arizona, developed EchoKick, a competitive social media environment that encourages sustainable and green choices.

- Students at Cab Calloway School of the Arts in Wilmington, Delaware, created VirDoc, a virtual cadaver for students to dissect while learning anatomy.

- A team of high school students at Tri-Tech Skills Center in Kennewick, Washington, invented Safe & Sound, an app that offers teens ways to manage stress and feelings of depression.

Google Science Fair winners ("Previous Years," n.d.) were limited only by their imagination:

- Fourteen-year-old Mihir Garimella of Pittsburgh, Pennsylvania, mimicked the evasion behavior of fruit flies in his flying sensor robot, enabling it to avoid collisions that could interfere with its work during disaster relief missions.

- Maya Varma, a fifteen-year-old student in San Jose, California, designed a low-cost apparatus for diagnosing lung disease. She 3D-printed a custom spirometer (an instrument for measuring the air capacity of the lungs) and associated it with a microprocessor and smartphone app, both of which she programmed. Her invention cost $35, the software is open source, and it helps diagnose five common respiratory illnesses.

Need more inspiration? These 2015 Intel International Science and Engineering Fair ("Intel International Science and Engineering Fair awards," n.d.) finalists tackled personal health and safety issues:

- Timothy Fossum Renier, age seventeen, of East High School, Duluth, Minnesota, knows that hand hygiene is key to preventing hospital-acquired infections. He programmed a Raspberry Pi minicomputer to monitor hand washing among hospital staff.

- Jaime Angel Hernandez and Aleida Olvera, juniors at Veterans Memorial Early College High School in Brownsville, Texas, invented SmartGuard, a wristband and smartphone app that alerts emergency contacts if something happens to the wearer.

- In a project called "Nuts to 911," Katherine Schweikert, a high school junior from Massachusetts Academy of Math & Science, engineered an enhancement to the EpiPen® (used to treat allergic reactions). She built and programmed a circuit board to pair the EpiPen with a smartphone. Pushing the EpiPen syringe activates the phone to auto-dial emergency services.

Where might your students' concerns and imagination take them? Even if they aren't ready to design full-blown solutions right now, encourage design thinking (Chapter 12) and give students exposure to the tools of invention—computers and programming.

IT WOULD BE IRRESPONSIBLE NOT TO INTRODUCE COMPUTER SCIENCE

Up to this point we've presented CS as a fundamental literacy, shared some of the amazing things kids accomplish with code, and presented the case that all young people should have the opportunity to learn. Let's pull back the lens a bit and consider, beyond the personal case, why it's important that CS becomes as common in the school curriculum as reading, writing, and math.

We all stand to benefit when more—and more kinds of—people get involved in technology. Presently, as a class offered in only a quarter of our high schools and often as an elective, CS reaches only a small subset of students. This group, predominantly white, middle class, and male, is insufficient to fill demand in the booming world of technology. We need a larger and more diverse talent pool from which to draw.

When work teams have diverse membership, they are more innovative and produce better products. This was borne out in a study of patents that looked at team composition and how highly regarded their patents were held (Ashcraft & Breitzman, 2012).

Patents awarded for information technology inventions over the past 25 years were examined and rated by the number of *subsequent* patents that cited them. It turns out that technology patents produced by mixed-gender teams received up to 42% more citations than those of their single-gender counterparts! This study noted only gender, but studies of diversity along race and cultural lines show the same effect. The "secret sauce" of varied perspectives and life experiences adds up to greater innovation, which benefits everyone.

Let's take a look at the video game industry. It might surprise you to know that female gamers over the age of 18 outnumber male gamers under the age of 18 by two to one ("2015 Essential Facts," 2015). A full 44% of all gamers are women, and they spend approximately 9.2 billion dollars on video games each year, yet the video game industry continues to target teenage males with their big label games and high-priced marketing campaigns. Why is this? In no small part, this has to do with the fact that 89% of game designers (and a whopping 97% of game programmers) are male (Burrows, 2013)!

Interestingly, though 94% of African American teens are active on social media, only 1.8% of all people who work at the most popular social media organizations are black (Harkinson, 2015). The story is much the same for Latinos and Latinas.

Entire groups of people are not getting the chance to participate in the creation of the environment where they spend so much time. Your instinct may be to ask why we should disrupt this trend if no one is complaining, and that's a popular question among those who benefit from the skewed metrics. The answer is, people *are* complaining, and lack of diversity is affecting more about the industry than the average CEO recognizes.

Diversify and Improve the Bottom Line

Until recently, the conversation around participation in fields where women and other groups are underrepresented centered on the issue of fairness. It's only *fair* that everyone has access to high-paying, creative jobs like those found in technology. This is true, but the value proposition goes deeper and beyond the individual. As the patent story illustrates, diversity improves innovation, and innovation affects our social fabric. We need more—and more kinds of—minds tackling our problems and improving our products and services.

Corporations know hiring more minorities and women is not just the fair and socially responsible thing to do. Products are better and market share is greater when solutions come from teams that reflect the customer base. Simply put, having a diverse workforce is competitive and improves the bottom line.

Diversify for a Bigger and Better Talent Pool

Another reason diversity matters? There are too few people taking up tech careers, and the gap between preparedness and opportunity is widening. By 2024 there will be 1.1 million computing-related job openings in the United States. At the present rate of preparation, we will be able to fill only 42% of those that require an undergraduate degree ("NCWIT by the Numbers," 2016).

By preparing more women and people of color, the talent pool will be not only more diverse but much larger. In fact, if women were involved in tech to the same degree as men, the persistent employment gap would be resolved.

> By 2024 there will be 1.1 million computing-related job openings in the United States. At the present rate of preparation, we will be able to fill only 42% of those that require an undergraduate degree.

Jobs Pay Well

Tech jobs pay well, and everyone should have access to high-wage jobs. Whether one has a technical certification, associate's degree, military experience, or a bachelor's degree, salaries in tech are higher than most jobs requiring the same amount of study or training. Table 2.1 provides a few examples from the U.S. Bureau of Labor Statistics (2015).

TABLE 2.1 Median Pay, 2014

JOB TITLE	DEGREE	2014 MEDIAN PAY
Computer support specialist	Associate or certificate	$50,380
Web developer	Associate	$63,490
Network systems administrator	Bachelor	$75,790
Computer programmer	Associate or Bachelor	$77,550
Software developer	Bachelor	$98,430

Source: U.S. Bureau of Labor Statistics (2015, December 17). 2014 Median Pay. Retrieved from http://www.bls.gov/ooh/computer-and-information-technology/home.htm

Fourteen of the twenty-five highest paying, most in-demand jobs available to people with a bachelor's degree are technical (Adams, 2015), and robust hiring is expected to continue into 2022.

Jobs Are Everywhere, Including in Your Hometown

Many think all tech jobs are in Silicon Valley or in tech hubs in large cities. Not so! Fully half of tech jobs are outside what we think of as the tech sector. Because technology is the backbone of commerce, health services, manufacturing, finance, and other major industries, a person can find a job in almost any industry anywhere in the country (or world) or close to home.

Technology-dependent companies you might not think of as technology companies are posting jobs like these on Dice.com, a jobs posting website for information technology and engineering professionals:

- UPS in Kentucky is seeking application architects and Java developers.
- John Deere in Illinois is looking for mobile app developers, IT analysts, and a Java tech lead.
- Macy's in New York is seeking e-commerce platform and mobile app developers.
- Bank of America in North Carolina is looking for software engineers, database administrators, and cyber security architects.
- Allstate Insurance in Arizona is hiring software developers and senior data scientists.
- Merck Pharmaceuticals seeks a laboratory information technology (IT) analyst in New Jersey, a database engineer in Prague, and a data security analyst in Singapore.
- Etsy, the online crafts marketplace, is looking for a user experience lead in Paris and a web operations manager in Dublin.

These Jobs Can Change the World

If someone had told me that software is really about humanity, that it's really about helping people by using computer technology, it would have changed my outlook earlier.

—Vanessa Hurst, founder, CodeMontage
(Lieberman & Chilcott, 2013)

Whether you're trying to make a lot of money or whether you just want to change the world, computer programming is an incredibly empowering skill to learn.

—Hadi Partovi, tech entrepreneur, investor,
and founder of Code.org
(Lieberman & Chilcott, 2013)

You probably know many young people who express an interest in careers that will make the world a better place. Tell every budding veterinarian, artist, business tycoon, humanitarian, health care provider, astronaut, and community activist you know that CS can be the "super power" they use to change the world.

Part 2

Casting Call

Join the growing crowd of teachers who are stepping up to computer science. You'll be ready for your close-up in no time.

3

Try Your Hand at Coding

Now that you have some sense of what coding, programming, and computer science (CS) are about, let's jump into some experiential learning. In this chapter, we encourage you to hop into some challenges, ignoring (for now) the practical application to teaching and learning in your classroom. Think of this instead as an open call, an opportunity to join the cast of this production called Computer Science!

As with almost any subject, the best way to learn CS deeply is to prepare to teach it. In many cases, the first step toward feeling comfortable teaching something new is to have some positive personal experiences with it. In our opinion, the best way to ensure a positive personal experience with CS is to start at the very beginning.

TIME WELL SPENT

In the remainder of this chapter, we walk you through a few exercises that, as they progress, increase in both complexity and ultimate reward. You may feel tempted to take a pass on preliminary activities, as they may seem trivial or overly simple. Be advised that these opportunities are worth your time. Just like a pre-workout stretch helps you stay limber and avoid injury, these exercises get you ready for learning in the chapters ahead. Additionally, it's quite likely that most of your students will be starting this adventure from scratch, so going through this process yourself will help you be an empathetic facilitator of their experience.

Because we respect your time, we considered a great assortment of tutorials before distilling our set down to three warm-ups and two exercises that will prepare you best for the chapters that follow.

To keep tabs on your thoughts, feelings, concerns, and questions, we urge you to grab a notebook or a digital tablet. Take note of your experience with each activity and write down questions as they come up. If those questions aren't answered in the remainder of this book, then use our companion site, resources.corwin.com/ComputationalThinking or Facebook page (facebook.com/groups/CodingInClass) to get them answered. If you are involved in a book study, share your notes about your experiences with your fellow readers, too. Keeping this experience collaborative is a big part of the fun.

KEY STRATEGY: PAIR PROGRAMMING

If you really want to make an impact as you go through the following exercises, we recommend pair programming. Pair programming is a proven method for both enhancing learning and writing better code. Sometimes called "peer programming," it is the act of coding with another person by your side. In schools, this happens by seating two students at the same machine and designating one person as the "driver" and the other as the "navigator." The driver works the mouse and keyboard—typing and maneuvering through the project—while the navigator pays attention to the big picture and makes sure that the code seems logical. The pair works like this for a short time (often by time limit, number of problems solved, or some other measurable mark); then they switch places.

It's easy to see the benefits of pair programming in an educational setting. First, pair programming helps teachers to accommodate an entire classroom with half as many machines. Also, students in both roles are thinking aloud, which is a metacognitive strategy for evaluating and improving reasoning. As an added bonus, the fact that each group has its own built-in sounding board cuts down on the number of hands being raised for teacher assistance (Williams, Kessler, Cunningham, & Jeffries, 2000). This means that students are also less likely to quit in frustration and are more likely to have fewer bugs in their resulting program (Williams & Upchurch, 2001).

The data surrounding pair programming is so strong that some companies have adopted it professionally. Often incorporated as part of an "extreme programming" mentality, studies show that these programming pairs turn out code of significantly higher quality in nearly the same amount of time as if each of the individuals had been working on his or her own. Besides, it's nice to have a buddy to bounce your ideas off of, and this method offers an environment for encouragement when a task seems overly daunting.

For all of the previously mentioned reasons, as well as the desire to spread CS to every classroom in the nation, we suggest that you go through the following exercises with a partner. If you're unable to find someone who can physically sit with you at your machine, arrange a Google Hangout,* and share your screen as you go. It's more than twice as nice to have another person to talk to and think aloud with as you progress through these activities.

❝*Alone we can do so little, together we can do so much.* ❞

—Helen Keller, author and activist

Now that you're prepared, it's time to jump in. As with any good workout, we'll start you with some warm-ups and stretches before we move to the main exercises. Give each a thorough try. As you go, take notes about your experiences, and consider the journal questions that follow each warm-up or exercise before you move from one to the next.

TEACHER WARM-UPS AND EXERCISES

Set aside a couple of hours to dig in to these warm-ups and exercises with a partner. Start at the beginning of the list, and move through sequentially, devoting 15 to 30 minutes to each. Every activity helps you build skills, confidence and familiarity that you will draw on as you read the rest of the book.

Warm-ups	
Warm-up 1: Magic Pen—Learn to think differently *(Play for 15–20 minutes)*	 **http://goo.gl/ Y8puxq**
Description: This flash-based physics game challenges a user to solve puzzles with only their magical pen and a library of shapes. Use this application to contemplate multiple solutions to difficult problems. The solutions are limited only by your imagination.	
Computer Science Tie-in: Break up the long vignettes into shorter puzzles using decomposition. See if you can find similarities between obstacles using pattern matching; then repurpose a previous solution with new details by abstracting out differences. Be persistent!	
Journal Questions • *How did you feel at the start of Magic Pen compared to after a few levels?* • *When you hit your first point of frustration, were you tempted to give up?* • *What kind of pep talk did you give yourself to persist a little longer?*	
http://media.abcya.com/games/magic_pen/flash/magic_pen.swf	

Warm-up 2: Play Auditorium—Persistence and debugging
(Play for 15–20 minutes)

http://goo.gl/
HQQfQD

Description: With beautiful streams of light and peaceful harmonies tinkling as you play, you will hardly realize how fast your pulse races as the level of difficulty increases. Every puzzle has a solution, but they are far from obvious.

Computer Science Tie-in: This is the ultimate test of persistence! Hang in there as you pass from challenge to challenge, debugging along the way. After each move, interpret the results to figure out what to do next. Are you getting closer to or further away from a solution?

Journal Questions

- *Was Auditorium all trial and error, or were you able to read the game's clues?*
- *At what points did you find yourself stopping to think and plan before proceeding?*
- *In what ways was it helpful to have another person go through the levels with you?*
- *Did "thinking aloud" help you combine your reasoning to get to the correct solution?*

http://www.cipherprime.com/games/auditorium

Warm-up 3: Lightbot—Using the computer to program
(Play for 15–20 minutes)

http://goo.gl/
54dWWK

Description: You'll be coding before you even know what's happening with this fun and friendly online game. Use instruction blocks such as a spring to jump and arrow to move forward as you navigate your lightbot among the squares to get to specific goal spaces.

Computer Science Tie-in: This application is intended to help you get used to dragging blocks to control the actions of your character and to learn how the process of calling functions enhances a program.

Journal Questions

- *Do you see how your activities relate to programming?*
- *In what ways did intuition help you progress?*
- *How did talking through the problems and even gesturing contribute to your progress through the levels?*

http://lightbot.com

Exercises

Exercise 1: CS Fundamentals Course 1—Vocabulary and concepts *(Play for 30–45 minutes)*

Description: This step-by-step tutorial is a true introduction to the basics of CS. You will learn about algorithms, debugging, persistence, loops, and events in this bona fide CS curriculum! Try to go as far as you can with this introductory course.

(You can skip the "unplugged" lessons, but take note of them for later.)

Computer Science Tie-in: Use this application to get familiar with CS vocabulary and concepts, and learn how to combine foundational elements like conditionals and events to solve tricky problems.

Journal Questions

- *You're programming! How does it feel?*
- *Were you able to get the hang of the block-based programming style?*
- *Did you get to experience loops and events?*
- *How might this be helpful when learning other concepts, like functions and variables?*

http://studio.code.org/s/course1

http://goo.gl/ OVGtsA

Exercise 2: Javascript.com by Code School—Practically programming *(Play for 30–45 minutes)*

Description: A smooth walk into text-based coding, this tutorial is a precursor to Code School's JavaScript Road Trip. Follow the directions to learn the basics of JavaScript, a powerful and flexible language for HTML and the web.

Computer Science Tie-in: Experience the beauty of typing lines of code into the console and watching your computer respond to your commands. This is the last step before preparing to write entry-level apps of your own.

Journal Questions

- *What was it like to control the computer with a language that is currently popular in the industry?*
- *Were you able to start picking up clues about some of the rules (such as putting quotes around strings of characters or using semicolons at the end of statements)?*
- *Can you imagine writing a program on your own, from the very beginning, or are you more inclined at this stage to continue building from a program that already has a framework?*

http://www.javascript.com

http://goo.gl/ RhMF3m

Summary	
In Summary: Journal and Share—Post to Facebook group	
Description: Summary reflection of warm-ups and exercises	
Journal Questions • *What is your overall impression of "programming?"* • *Were you able to think of these tasks as puzzles and challenges, or did they feel like homework?* • *Which activity made you the most excited, and why?* • *Which really tested you, and how did you feel about feeling uncertain at times?* • *What would you tell someone else about your first experiences?*	https://goo.gl/ h6P7NC
https://www.facebook.com/groups/CodingInClass	

What Have I Done and What Do I Do Next?

This chapter has taken you on a long journey from the place of a lone educator exploring the possibility of incorporating CS into the classroom to that of an entry-level programmer! Now that you've had a taste, take a moment to pat yourself on the back. Celebrate a bit, then dive into the next chapter, where we start imagining what CS could look like as part of a well-rounded classroom curriculum. Lights, camera, action!

4

Getting Started in the Classroom

As a teacher, you don't have to look far to find concerns when it comes to integrating computer science into everyday instruction. You or your colleagues may be concerned about fitting one more piece of curriculum into an already crowded program. Parents worry about adding more "screen time" to a child's routine. School administrators aren't certain computer science is worth the cost of retraining teachers.

The trick, and moral responsibility, is to integrate computer science activities in a way that elevates the "pros" while diminishing the "cons" so students get the experiences they need.

When adding computer science to your plan, you can keep many issues under control with a simple gut check. Do students find all the computational activities interesting? If not, some may be overused. Do the activities enhance a science investigation or creative process? Creating a computer model or simulation can help your students to see or experience information in a way that is otherwise impossible, and the possibilities for digital art are endless. If your answers all fall on the side of enhanced student experience, then you're on the right track!

START LOW-TECH

One way computer science can be integrated into the classroom without additional screen time is through "unplugged" activities. Unplugged lessons are computer science activities that do not require digital devices or the internet. Consider them the "live theater" of CS! Often, they involve arts, crafts, games, and movement to get across vocabulary and concepts as complex and diverse as you might find in an entry-level college class. Showing is easier than telling, so give one of our "unplugged" lessons (like "Algorithms and Automation—A Compliment Generator" on p. 76), and peruse the companion site for links to some of our favorites.

ENCOURAGE MOVEMENT

Part of being a responsible CS educator is teaching your students how to be responsible CS learners. This means students need to think about taking care of their bodies, their minds, and their environment.

When it comes to the body, the use of technology can take its toll. Sitting at a computer for long periods is not good for anyone's health. Encourage kids to get up and walk around often, especially when programming on a machine. Allowing students to walk freely about the room to study what others are doing might be frowned on in math class, but in computer science, active collaboration is an effective learning technique.

Computer activity should take place in small chunks of time, ideally for no longer than you would expect students to be able to sit and read on their own without interruption. Why? Well, when we are out in the world, humans usually look around in three-dimensional (3D) space with nearly 180 degrees of range top to bottom, and side to side. When on a computer, we focus only on a 2D space with a range of about 30 degrees top to bottom and 40 to 50 degrees side to side ("Monitor Height and Position Guidelines," 2008). Spending too much time in this limited, high-contrast atmosphere can cause eye strain and muscle soreness. With this in mind, encourage students to follow the 20/20/20 Rule: Every 20 minutes, get up and stretch while looking at least 20 feet away for at least 20 seconds. Set a timer if you need to.

> 20/20/20/ Rule: Every 20 minutes, get up and stretch while looking at least 20 feet away for at least 20 seconds.

These breaks are a great opportunity for conversation, too. If you want to give students' full bodies a break, maybe some dance moves are in order! The Tut, Clap, Jive activity that we refer to on page 51 would be fun day after day.

Issues of sedentary living extend beyond school, of course. Teach students that for each hour of screen time they have in a day, they should spend the same amount of time outside playing, engaging in sports, or just going for a restorative stroll. If they begin to hear this encouragement early, being active has a much better chance of becoming a habit than if they only hear it later in life.

When it comes to technology, it's your job to help students manage their own well-being. Now that we've covered the physical bit, it's time to talk about mental steadfastness as it relates to the digital world.

FOSTER CRITICAL CONSUMPTION

A recent report from the United Kingdom ("Children and Parents: Media Use and Attitudes Report," 2015) shows that students are increasingly believing everything they read on the internet. This problem is probably compounded by the likelihood that their parents believe everything *they* read on the internet, too, and pass the information along. To exacerbate things further, intelligent search engines (like Google) have tuned their algorithms to the point where they offer "top results" based on known preferences (Herlocker, Dietterich, Forbes, & Maritz, 2012), so the "best" results for any search you create will tend to be consistent with whatever viewpoint you already have (White, 2013).

In the same way, social media sites like Facebook saturate your feed with posts from friends that you interact with the most, making it all but certain that the majority of viewpoints that you're exposed to will continue to fuel your existing beliefs.

This is a great time for solidarity, but an awful time for the open-minded exploration of differing points of view. For that reason, every student should receive a thorough education on the credibility of the web. While not explicitly computer science, the care and proper use of search engines is important to CS education, and therefore, it is important to discuss in this book.

It helps for students to recognize that, like movies, web pages can seem authentic and still be entirely fictitious. Even after this message has been absorbed, there is power and authority in published words from other sources. It is worth taking your students through some exercises where they see how ludicrous even some of the most believable pages are. Teach them how to "check their work" in the same way that they might for math class. Have them take a "fact" and trace it back somewhere other than Wikipedia. Is one of the first results on the page from Snopes.com?

Truly educated citizens need to understand where their facts are coming from, and while we gave you a small taste of the need to learn about our sources of information, it would require another book entirely to do the subject justice. Please see our companion website (resources.corwin.com/ComputationalThinking) for more details around lessons in this subject.*

"People are very gullible. They'll believe anything they see in print. **"**

—E. B. White, *Charlotte's Web*

PROTECT PRIVACY AND PREVENT CYBERBULLYING

It is said that "familiarity breeds contempt," but apparently anonymity breeds disregard, criticism, and hostility. A study by the University of

Houston found that anonymous users were nearly twice as likely to post uncivil comments than users who were somehow required to identify themselves (53.3% to 28.8%, respectively; Santana, 2013). This explains a lot of the horrid behavior on the internet.

Digital divide: Inequalities perpetuated by disparate access to computers and the internet.

Students today have it hard enough straddling the **digital divide** with the pressure to be carrying the newest, best device. When you add anonymous internet interactions to the mix, it creates the stuff of teenage nightmares. Since roughly 91% of all teens access the internet from a mobile device, and nearly 71% of all teens frequent more than one social media site (Lenhart, 2015), it's almost certain that each of them will run into haters at some point.

If not monitored properly, the internet can be turned into a psychological weapon ("The Top Six Unforgettable Cyberbullying Cases," 2013) full of venom and danger. So what is an educator to do when encouraging students to browse and share on a regular basis?

Up to Age 13: Monitor and Protect

Most students younger than age 13 are not allowed to have their own accounts on social media in the United States. If you are using blogs or online learning sites in your classroom, make sure that you are in control of setting up each account. Educational sites for children (like Codecademy, Code.org, and Edublogs) will generally have bulk sign-up pages to associate students with your teacher account without sharing too much personal information, such as student IDs or email addresses.

If you are using sites that require individual emails for students, try creating a single Gmail address for each class; then append numbers to the end of it when signing up each student. For instance, if we made the Gmail address k!k!Class@gmail.com, then we could use k!k!Class+1@gmail.com for the first student, k!k!Class+2@gmail.com for the second student, and so on. Every message that came through to any of those accounts would then be delivered to you at the main k!k!Class@gmail.com account.

Age 13 and Older: Trust but Verify

Teenagers and the internet are a tumultuous combination. Teens are old enough to be treated with autonomy and trust, but they are still testing boundaries and challenging consequences. As an educator, how do you strike a balance?

At this age, we recommend that you work with their desire to express themselves and encourage appropriate use of social media in study and as a portfolio medium for their accomplishments. Be open about the pitfalls of posting on a forum that allows comments from the general public, and encourage students to protect their privacy by allowing only personal friends to access their profiles. Round out the topic by giving a name to cyberbullying and condemning it outright, with zero tolerance and well-defined ramifications. Follow up the conversation by describing what to do when a student believes he or she has been the target of a bully online (Cyberbullying Research Center, n.d.).

No matter what age your students are, talk to them about being good digital citizens and respecting others, even when their identity is hidden. Remind students that the true measure of one's character is what they do when no one is looking. Challenge them to defend their own accounts and protect those of others. If your students are prepared to make good choices, then when the time comes to act, they just might do the right thing.

If you aren't already steeped in your district's acceptable use practices (AUPs), look them up and respond accordingly. If you'd like a deeper dive into digital safety and citizenship, read *Digital Citizenship in Schools,* by Mike Ribble (ISTE, 2015).

ACHIEVE ACCESS

Teachers often cite two hurdles when it comes to incorporating computer science into their classroom: time and budget restrictions. Both of these can be addressed by selecting the right curriculum for your classroom.

Computer science can be introduced into multiple subjects even without having entire classes devoted to the subject. The truth is, computer science is the understanding of computing as a tool, and that tool can be used in service to any subject. At young ages, Scratch gives you a tool to bring CS into music (Heines, Ruthmann, Greher, & Maloney, 2012), CS Fundamentals allows you to use computer science in art ("Computer Science Fundamentals for Elementary School," 2015), and Tynker brings computer science into math class ("Programming = Better Math Skills + Fun," 2014).

For middle school and beyond, entire organizations are dedicated to interdisciplinary computing, including Bootstrap (math) and Project GUTS (science), which we point to in Chapter 16.

What's more, when students become capable of understanding text-based programming languages, their world opens up with opportunities for CS integration. Imagine students going deeper with projects by adding formulas to spreadsheets, adding interactivity to maps, and creating graphical representations from data.

The cost of equipping a school is nominal for most of the programs listed earlier. Many of the curriculum packages mentioned are free, and some providers even offer free professional development opportunities for educators. Functional equipment becomes the next consideration, but these costs can be mitigated through pair programming (because half as many machines are needed), more agile, on-demand access to school technology (as schools dismantle computer labs and supply more computers to classrooms), and adoption of BYOD ("bring your own device") policies.

Programming environment: A software workspace made for creating code.

For the cases where classrooms are unable to procure hardware capable of running up-to-date browsers, unplugged CS lessons are the next best option. Many, like Conditionals with Cards* or For Loop Fun* use only paper, playing cards, and/or dice.

Suppose, however, that you are one of the lucky ones, and you have found the time and the hardware to implement a full-scale computer science program. You may worry that it's like the old days when coding meant installing complicated **programming environments** and dozens of **software patches**, but have no fear. Today, many great entry-level programming environments are browser-based and operate online, allowing your students to receive the benefits of an introductory CS education through a handful of quality websites.

Software patch: A piece of software designed to update or fix a computer program.

BANISH ANXIETY

In reality, we have found that the biggest barrier to providing students with a solid introduction to computer science is teacher anxiety.

Worry not, brave instructor, because the most important thing that you can teach in CS is how to learn, and you can model this as you learn alongside your students. Computer science changes fast. A programming language introduced to students their first year of high school might be outdated by the time they graduate. Even the most learned computer science professor doesn't have enough CS knowledge to answer every stray question from an elementary student. For this reason, we ask that you become comfortable saying, "Let's find out together."

Adopt the motto, "Everyone a teacher, everyone a learner." Students solidify their learning when they teach someone else (Brooks & Brooks, 1993), so let them end a lesson by teaching you and their classmates what they discovered. This is a great opportunity to challenge students to put what they've learned—and how they learned it—into words. Thinking through their actions not only helps them accomplish the day's task but it exposes the processes of learning something new; a skill that can transfer to every learning challenge they encounter for the rest of their lives.

If you are used to dispensing knowledge and controlling most aspects of the learning experience, give yourself permission to let go—even if for only one group of kids around one topic. We promise the experience will be both enlightening and enriching for everyone involved.

"_Have no fear of perfection—you'll never reach it._**"**

—Salvador Dali, artist

5

Dos and Don'ts of Teaching Computer Science

We've just spent a chapter navigating issues and addressing concerns. Now it's time to get to the nitty-gritty of how to make computer science (CS) work in your classroom. We'll start with some "dos" and "don'ts."

1. *DON'T* EXPECT TO BE AN EXPERT

With the current state of CS education, it is very rare to find true expert teachers, especially in Grades K–8. Only a handful of them exist, and many have been kidnapped by well-intentioned organizations to help them figure out how to produce more experts in CS education! Instead of focusing on learning everything about CS before you take your first step, dive in *with* your students. Use your powers of facilitation to promote inquiry. Demonstrate "think aloud" strategies as you model problem solving, and resiliency as you try one approach and then another. Don't show students where they go wrong, but ask, "What happened?" Follow up with questions such as:

- "What are you trying to accomplish?"
- "What did you try?"
- "Why do you think that didn't work?"
- "What does that tell you?"
- "What could you try next?"

2. *DO* LET YOUR CLASS EXPLORE

Exploration is a powerful learning process. It's so much more than just guess and check. When students are allowed to explore the reactions to and consequences of their own creations, they start to understand the environment better than they ever could by just having you explain the lay of the land. Exploring allows them to chart a map in their head of the places that they can go and the mechanisms they can use to solve the problems at hand. Learning is far more meaningful when students form their own questions via hands-on work (Friesen & Scott, 2013).

3. *DO* LET YOUR CLASS SHARE

This suggestion has two meanings. First, having students work in isolation would be a false (and dreary) reflection of the way CS is done in the real world. No professional is expected to come up with solutions by their lonesome, and if programmers refused to use the plethora of resources on the Internet in favor of creating their own code from scratch, they would probably be fired for inefficiency. Computer science is collaborative and exploratory. There are many ways to solve any given problem. Learning is most effective when students are able to see how other people tackle an issue, then are able to step back and analyze why and how the solution worked, to see if they can incorporate pieces of it into their own project. It's not always about pulling answers out of thin air. More often than not, it's about learning to learn from peers and learning to explain their solution to others.

Second, we should nurture students' sense of pride in their unique contributions. Unlike math or spelling where everyone gets the same correct answer to a specific problem, CS allows for a range of diverse and creative processes and outcomes. Allow students to share their projects. Whether sharing with you, the class, or to their families and friends through social media, students deserve to show the impact of their work.

4. *DO* GIVE KIDS TIME TO MOVE

Classroom management often begins with the idea that kids need to be quietly seated. This "sit down and quiet down" mentality is great for a teacher's sanity, but it's rough on collaboration and morale. During CS lessons, especially when pair programming, students should be communicating constantly. The happier and more excited they are, the more animated they're going to become. Students will need help from time to time, and we suggest using the "Try Three, Then Three, Then Me" strategy. With this hybrid help method, students must attempt a task three times before they seek help from a neighboring group. That group must work with the students, then try and fail three *more* times before asking for help from the teacher.

This has several benefits. The first is that it encourages persistence. Students will train themselves to chug through and solve little problems instead of stopping in their tracks until help arrives. Second, it gives students a chance to move around the room with purpose (going to help a neighbor). Third, students are getting involved in each other's work, learning from and being inspired by one another. Finally, this means less overall classroom chaos, as fewer kids will have their hands in the air calling for you, risking boredom and misbehavior while they wait. A brave teacher may even take the need for movement one step further and build in breaks using a site like GoNoodle* (gonoodle.com). An interactive website with calming, energizing, and stretching activities, it can either help students feel more centered or allow them to blow off steam. One step down from that might be giving the students permission to walk quietly around the room to see what everyone else is doing when they start to get antsy. Not only will that give them a stretch break, but it could also help get them unstuck or give them a chance to unstick a classmate.

5. *DO* GET CREATIVE

There is room in almost any class for a CS project. Whether you're an elementary school teacher who wants to inject some interactivity into language arts* or a middle school teacher who wants to bring historical maps to life,* one class period is often all you need to get your students off and running. Don't fall into the trap of thinking that you need to teach an entire semester of curriculum or nothing at all. Of course, more would be better, but even a taste of programming gives students the exposure they need to make informed choices later in life.

6. *DON'T* BE A BORE

You *can* do this wrong. Over and over again, we have to remind educators that CS education *can* do more harm than good to a child's **self-efficacy**. It's not the challenge that will make students decide that they're not suited for future CS explorations. On the contrary! It's often boredom and confusion. If you indicate that you're not interested in CS, your students won't be either. Take some of that love of learning that got you into teaching in the first place and learn right alongside your class. Create projects with them. Squeal about your discoveries. Cheer about theirs. Forget that soggy notion that you have in your head about the crusty old professor spouting multisyllabic vocabulary in a musty classroom and replace it with a new image of you forging active, practical applications with your kids as you navigate the world of CS together. What do your students want to do? What resources do you need in order to help them do that? Does your end result always have to be a grade, or can it also be a website that helps track the location of local recycling plants? Could your students find more meaning in creating an application that everyone in

Self-efficacy:
A person's belief about his or her own abilities to learn, complete tasks, and reach goals.

“The computer is incredibly fast, accurate, and stupid. Man is incredibly slow, inaccurate, and brilliant. The marriage of the two is a force beyond calculation.”

—Leo Cherne

Are you starting to imagine what you and your students can accomplish with computer science?

Part 3

In Production

A lot goes into the production of computer software and other digital artifacts. The tools of the trade include computational thinking, programming, and supplies found in the makerspace. Just as getting the perfect shot on the film set can take many tries, so can perfecting the techniques that foster computational thinking and spatial reasoning. The chapters in Part 3 help set the scene for deep learning.

6

Activities That Foster Computational Thinking

THINKING COMPUTATIONALLY

As enthusiasm for computer science grows, so, too, does interest in helping students develop their computational thinking chops. We touched on the pillars of computational thinking in Chapter 1, and we will delve a little deeper here. You might be thinking, "Oh no! Is computational thinking another flavor-of-the week competency? Some specialized and arcane slice of intellect I'm supposed to nurture?" Fear not and bear with us. Before we dig in to the very practical nature of computational thinking, let's break apart and simplify to make sense of the concept more generally.

> Simply put, computational thinking is a set of skills that help to set up a problem in such a way that a computer can help you solve it.

Have you ever noticed the huge value put on problem *solving?* It's represented in all science, technology, engineering, and math (STEM) education standards; in the International Society for Technology in Education (ISTE) educational technology standards; and in the Computer Science Teacher Association (CSTA) standards as both a disposition and a skill. But what about problem *finding* and problem *posing?* Those are great intellectual challenges, too. Computational thinking ventures into this realm—sorting out what to pay attention to and how to frame a problem so that problem solving becomes part of a coherent progression. Computational thinking can lead to some kind of computing action, but as you'll see, it's a way of thinking that supports inquiry and problem posing and problem solving beyond the domains of computer science.

Educationally, the trick lies in figuring out how to effectively hone your students' computational thinking skills in a way that makes it obvious that computational thinking is helpful in every area of life. Computational thinking can be woven into any subject almost effortlessly. Trying to read a word that's too difficult? Use decomposition. Can't remember how to multiply 9 by 9? Look for a pattern when multiplying with easier numbers.

If we as educators get comfortable calling out thinking practices by name, students will begin to understand how useful they are. With practice, students can get to the point where they can figure out which element of computational thinking will help them with any given problem and begin to learn without explicitly being taught.

In every course that Kiki leads, no matter the age of the students, there comes a lesson that she refuses to teach. This isn't due to her diva-like nature, but rather her love for inspiring self-led learning and genuine inquiry. Years ago, Kiki would run multiple classes at the same time. One semester in particular, she had finished creating her "unplugged" lesson "It's Electric"* and decided to try it out with one of her second-grade groups—after other unplugged activities but before online programming. The entire premise of "It's Electric" is that students can teach themselves things just by forming questions and experimenting until they figure out the answers. At no point in this lesson is the instructor allowed to "teach," and the instructor lets the class know this right from the beginning. Here is how Kiki would usually kick this lesson off:

> *I know that you're all looking forward to making your own light sculptures today. It's going to be so much fun! You'll be discovering what to do all on your own. All I can tell you is that you get to take the battery-operated candle apart and use the other supplies to turn it into something new. That's it. I won't be helping with anything else!*
>
> *Now, there might come a moment when you get stuck, or you have a question, and you're going to say, "Ms. Kiki, Ms. Kiki, I'm stuck. I need help!" and I'm just going to say, "How exciting, that means you're ready to learn something!" You might ask, "Can you pleeeeeaaaase help me?" and I'm going to say, "Nope."*
>
> *You might even beg "PLEASE? I don't know what I'm doing!" and I'll say, "Neither does anyone else! No one expects you to know something that you haven't learned yet! Keep experimenting."*
>
> *You might think I'm rude, and mean, and that I don't care, but I promise you that I do. The reason that we're doing this today is to help you see that you don't need to be TAUGHT something to LEARN it!*

Even though this wasn't meant to be an experiment, something amazing happened. Once the classes moved into programming, the students who received this lesson were far less likely to get derailed by small hurdles. These students would try more things on their own and would persist far longer than the students who hadn't received a similar lesson.

Kiki has since paired an inquiry lesson with computational thinking in every course she runs at all grade levels. This combination gives students such power and confidence that phrases like "I don't get it" start to turn into "I just need to figure out why the cat is moving up instead of over."

DIGGING DEEPER INTO COMPUTATIONAL THINKING

Depending on the computational thinking resources you explore, you will find a variety of definitions, categories, and subskills. For our purposes, we'll focus on four commonly recognized pillars of computational thinking. Table 6.1 offers definitions and nontechnical examples of each, and the short chapters that follow offer a more thorough description and activities and lesson plans to try with your students.

TABLE 6.1 Computational Thinking-at-a-Glance

	DECOMPOSITION	PATTERN MATCHING	ABSTRACTION	AUTOMATION
Quick Definition	Breaking something down into smaller parts	Finding similarities between pieces	Generalizing the things that are different from each other	Plugging pieces into an algorithm to help with a result
Subcategories	Data analysis	Data visualization	Data modeling, pattern generalization	Algorithm design, parallelization, simulation
Nontechnical Examples	Trying to remember a phone number? Break it into three shorter pieces. Now the number doesn't seem so intimidating!	The light turns on when you flip the switch once, 3 times, or 5 times. It turns off when you flip it twice, 4 times, or 6 times. What state will the light be on after 8 flips?	1 truck has 4 wheels. 2 trucks have 8 wheels. 3 trucks have 12 wheels. X trucks have (X times 4) wheels.	Dishwashers automate the work of washing dishes. Whether it's a plate, a bowl, or a pan, you can put it in dirty and it comes out clean.

It may still seem hard to comprehend the precise time to use each of these pillars, and that's okay. It all comes with practice. In the chapters that follow, you will have a chance to see each computational thinking concept in action in some targeted activities.

7

Decomposition

The father of Taoism, Lao Tzu, is credited with saying that the "journey of a thousand miles begins with a single step," and that is just as true for computer science as for a long trek.

Any challenge can seem daunting if you try to take in the entire task at once. We've all had that sinking feeling that comes when a huge project is looming, but how much easier is it to take one step at a time? Imagine creating all of the costumes for a space movie. If you imagine the whole effort as a six-month-long nightmare, it may feel pretty daunting. If instead, you were to take it one costume piece at a time, focusing only on the work that goes into each component—first doing the helmets, then the suits, then the badges and patches—you would end up with a much simpler and more manageable process and fewer errors!

Decomposition is the magic that makes solving complicated problems possible. Simply put, decomposition is breaking a problem down into smaller, more manageable parts. Just the process of breaking a problem down can help a solution come to light, but even if it doesn't, it is much easier to look at a small series of steps than a large problem as a whole.

Often, it's best to identify your first step, but when the first move is unclear, try to figure out what step you need to make right before you finish and work backward until the rest of the solution emerges. Whichever way it goes, solving little subproblems can teach you quite a lot about the technique that you need to use to work out the big problem as a whole.

Take, for example, mathematical equations. Multiplication, as many of us learned to do it, is an example of decomposing and recombining. Unless using a calculator, 436×12 is a bit challenging to solve. It is much easier to solve it in little pieces, so we use long multiplication to break it into (436 × 2) + (436 × 10), which is 872 + 4360, which equals 5232.

$$
\begin{array}{r}
436 \\
* \ 12 \\
\hline
872 \\
\end{array} \ +
$$

$$
\begin{array}{r}
4360 \\
\hline
5232 \\
\end{array}
$$

In fact, the act of using parentheses in math is an example of decomposition, since parentheses are used to break a large problem into smaller parts.

If you practice no other elements of computational thinking (CT) for the rest of your life (which seems unlikely), practice decomposition eagerly and often. If you do, you'll find that many of the problems that vex your peers will seem like a manageable cluster of trivial things to you.

66 *When eating an elephant, take one bite at a time.* **99**

—Creighton Abrams, U.S. Army general

In this chapter, you will find a curated table of resources for learning more about decomposition, followed by a sample classroom lesson, "Break It Down!" The meaning and utility of decomposition will become clear in the context of the sample lesson, so give it a quick scan and imagine teaching "Break It Down!" to your students.

Decomposition Resources

Here are several lessons to examine, followed by a complete plan for "Break It Down!" a lesson that illustrates the concept—and value—of decomposition.

Tut, Clap, Jive by the Barefoot Programme *(Ages 5 and older, approx. 30 minutes)*	
"This is an unplugged activity in which pupils create hand clapping, hand tutting, or hand jive sequences of movements. Pupils break the sequence of actions down into parts and in so doing are decomposing. Pupils link this idea to breaking problems down when creating computer programs such as animations or games."	http://goo.gl/ 7RMSHI
http://barefootcas.org.uk/sample-resources/decomposition/ks12-introduction-decomposition-unplugged-activity	

Divide and Conquer by Google for Education *(Ages 11–14, approx. 45 minutes)*

https://goo.gl/ T0S9WT |
| "In this lesson, students will use a 'divide-and-conquer' strategy to solve the mystery of 'stolen crystals' using decomposition to break the problem into smaller problems and algorithmic design to plan a solution strategy." | |
| *https://docs.google.com/document/d/1DMDuomVc5gZ_NSaC3afERx40uES WweydMICqetin3to/edit?usp=sharing* | |

This lesson plan is available for download at resources.corwin.com/ ComputationalThinking.

Original Lesson

CT Focus: Decomposition	
Cross-Curricular Ties: Math	games.thinking myself.com
Age Range: 8–14	
Duration: 30 minutes	
Scan the QR Code or type the URL to see the online game that inspired this lesson.	

Overview

In this lesson, students learn the value of decomposition by breaking large problems into smaller, more manageable bites. Working together, students will receive puzzles that consist of a picture of a brick wall and a set of cardboard faces that can be used to create the bricks for that wall. Students must decompose the puzzle into single-unit problems where they can solve for one brick. After that, they'll apply the information they discovered to each of the subgroups they created until they have answered the puzzle as a whole.

Vocabulary

Decomposition: The process of breaking down a big problem into smaller pieces. Decomposition can help make solutions easier to see.

Lesson Objectives

Students will be able to:

- Break a large problem down into smaller parts
- Create math equations based on images
- Compute the number of items needed to construct an imaginary wall
- Describe in their own words how decomposition can make difficult problems easier to solve

Materials and Resources

- Paper
- Pencils
- Whiteboard or projector
- Puzzle cards

Preparation

1. Read the lesson and decide how it can best fits into the age range of your classroom.

2. Visit http://games.thinkingmyself.com and run through the section on "Decomposition" to illustrate the ideas behind this concept.

3. If students will be working in groups (Grades 3 and higher), print out enough puzzles for each group. If the whole class is working together, you can cut puzzles into individual sheets for use with overhead projection.

4. Consider bringing boxes (such as tissue boxes, cereal boxes, match boxes, or DVD cases) as a physical illustration of what students will be emulating.

Activity

Step 1. Introduction—Take a moment in front of the class to build a simple three-level pyramid. Just the act of doing this will likely grab students' attention. When your pyramid is complete, let students know that you have a puzzle for them.

> "I want to cover each side of each box with paper. I know I can get pieces of paper in exactly the right size to fit each side of each box, but they're really expensive, so I don't want to waste any. How many pieces of each size paper will I need to do all of these boxes?"

Illustrate with sample images of the paper sizes needed to cover one box (either draw on the board with dimensions included, or physically cut out).

Young students will likely start making wild guesses, while older students will probably start to do some mental math. Ask for volunteers with answers.

When you get a student with the correct answer, ask what steps he or she used to solve the problem. (He or she will likely have broken it down to something like "We have n [number of] boxes with 2 sides of x, 2 sides of y, and 2 sides of z.")

If your class doesn't get to a correct answer, start to pull the pyramid apart into individual groups for each row (one of 3, one of 2, and one of 1).

> "Here, does this help?"

Older students will most certainly get it at this point, while younger students will likely need to be walked through the practice of figuring it out for one box, then multiplying by two to get the answer for the second row, then multiplying by three to get the answer for the third row, and lastly, adding all of those numbers together.

What we just did is called **_decomposition_**! "Decomposing" is breaking something down into smaller pieces, and by using decomposition, we can get a puzzle down into its simplest problem and make quick work of solving it. Next, all we have to do is follow back through our decomposition process, building the problem back up step-by-step until we have a final answer!

Step 2. Play with puzzles—Students should now be excited to try these puzzles on their own. Go through one or two examples with them before you turn them loose, to be sure that students understand that they should be breaking the puzzles down gradually instead of jumping straight from the wall to the individual bricks (see Figure 7.1). This will make it easier to get the final answer when they start putting everything back together.

For young students, use tally marks to keep track of sides, and then count for final answers. Grades 3 and higher should be able to handle using quantities (see Figures 7.2–7.4).

Breakdown:

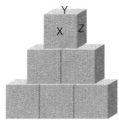

How many pieces
do we need of each size?

X _____
Y _____
Z _____

FIGURE 7.1 Older Student Demo

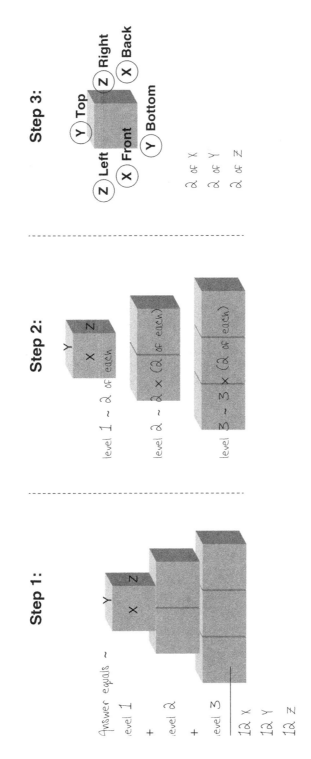

Step 1:

Answer equals ~

level 1

+

level 2

+

level 3

_____

12 X
12 Y
12 Z

Step 2:

Y
X
Z

level 1 ~ 2 of each

level 2 ~ 2 × (2 of each)

level 3 ~ 3 × (2 of each)

Step 3:

(Z) Left (Y) Top
(X) Front (Z) Right
(Y) Bottom (X) Back

2 of X
2 of Y
2 of Z

FIGURE 7.2 Decomposing the Bricks Problem

Be sure to explain to students whether you intend for them to write directly on the puzzles or if they should use additional sheets of paper.

Challenge students to come up with extra puzzles for each other when they've finished the examples on the worksheet.

Step 3. Share—Ask students to chat in their groups about the puzzles that they solved. Which was most difficult? Why? What other places in life can students see that breaking a problem down into smaller pieces would make the problem easier to solve?

Step 4. Discuss together—Bring the class back together for a chat.

- Were these problems easier to solve in one glance, or after breaking them into pieces?
- Were there times when it was fine to jump from the whole puzzle down to one brick instantly and then do the math to solve just once?
- Were there times that it was easiest to break the big puzzle down into many subgroups before solving for a single brick? How did that make it easier to solve the whole puzzle?
- Where are some other places in your life that you could use decomposition to make problem solving easier?

What It's All About

In the real world, computer scientists use decomposition all the time. They often get clients who want them to build very large and complex programs. To understand what a big project will take, these pros need to break it down into lots of little elements, so they can figure out how to approach the code. Often, when it's time to program the application, the engineers will break those pieces into even smaller chunks (called *procedures*) to help keep everything as clean and simple as possible.

This lesson plan is available for download at resources.corwin.com/ComputationalThinking.

Example:

How many do we need of each size piece?

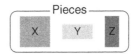

X _____
Y _____
Z _____

Puzzle 1:

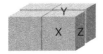

How many do we need of each size piece?

X _____
Y _____
Z _____

Puzzle 2:

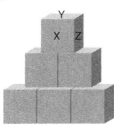

How many do we need of each size piece?

X _____
Y _____
Z _____

FIGURE 7.3 Decomposition Puzzles

This lesson plan is available for download at resources.corwin.com/
ComputationalThinking.

Puzzle 3:

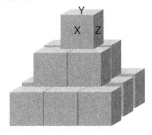

How many do we need
of each size piece?

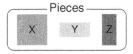

X _____
Y _____
Z _____

Puzzle 4:

How many do we need
of each size piece?

X _____
Y _____
Z _____

Puzzle 5:

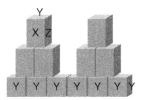

How many do we need
of each size piece?

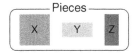

X _____
Y _____
Z _____

FIGURE 7.4 Harder Decomposition Puzzles

8

Pattern Recognition (With Pattern Matching)

At first glance, pattern recognition (including pattern matching) might seem extremely obvious, a skill that we've all mastered by the end of third grade. It's true that basic patterns jump right out at most of us: the repeated designs on wrapping paper, straightforward number sequences, the musical cacophony of a police siren . . . but once patterns stop being easy, we no longer recognize them instantly. This allows simple solutions for complex problems to hide in plain sight.

Pattern recognition, as a part of computational thinking (CT), is the practice of finding similarities between items as a way of gaining extra information. *Pattern matching* is more about the realization that something matches a pattern already "recognized," though you will often hear the terms used synonymously, since they are frequently used interchangeably in CT.

In Figure 8.1, you'll find three basic patterns. How quickly can you figure out what they are? How quickly can you come up with the next item in the series?

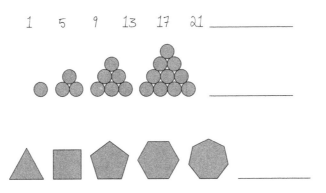

FIGURE 8.1 Three Basic Patterns

Figure 8.2 shows three more patterns. All rely on simple mathematics or life intuition that could be expected of an adult that has graduated from the American public school system, even though the sequences may not seem to be sequences at all! How long does it take before you can come up with the next item in each series?

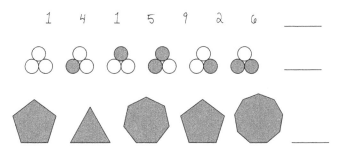

FIGURE 8.2 More Complex Patterns

It's likely evident to you that it only takes a small amount of additional complexity before we stop instantly comprehending sequences as patterns. Should you be wiggling with curiosity, you can find the answers for the second group of puzzles (and the logic behind them) at the end of this chapter.

One very entertaining mathematical pattern that can be easily witnessed in nature is called the Fibonacci series. Created by adding the current number to the number that came before it $n = (n{-}1 + n{-}2)$, the Fibonacci series builds a beautiful spiral that can be seen in the tines of a pinecone, the growth of a snail shell, or even the positioning of leaves on a tree Figure 8.3, p. 62.

n	1	2	3	4	5	6	7	8
Fib(n)	1	1	2	3	5	8	13	21

Table of numbers in the Fibonacci series: 1, 1, 2, 3, 5, 8, 13, 21, . . .

On its own, pattern matching can be useful for solving future puzzles that are similar in nature. This skill can be enhanced with practice, which leads to improvement in your ability to look at a problem, spot a familiar pattern, and intuit a solution. Pattern recognition can be associated with common acts like knowing how to open a new book or even being able to seamlessly hop from using one brand of phone to another.

As with the previous chapter on decomposition, we leave you with activities to explore and a lesson plan to try.

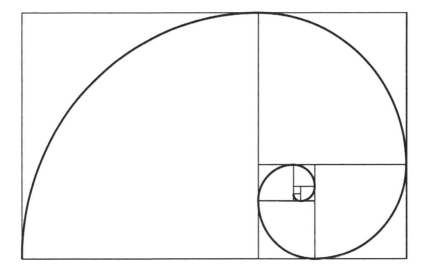

FIGURE 8.3 A Fibonacci spiral is where the length of sides represents sums of the sides of the two squares but grow smaller.

Source: Fibonacci, *Liber Abaci*, 1202

Pattern Recognition Resources	
Cut Block Logic Puzzles by Queen Mary University of London *(Age 11 and older, approx. 45 minutes)*	**https://goo.gl/ 1ZUu5S**
"Learn how to solve a logic puzzle and find out about why logical thinking is a core part of computational thinking. Discover how generalisation and pattern matching are the secret skills of experts, both in computer science and other areas too, from chess players to firefighters."	
https://teachinglondoncomputing.files.wordpress.com/2015/11/booklet-cutblocklogicpuzzles.pdf	

Cipher Sleuths curated by the National Security Agency *(Ages 9 and older, approx. 45 minutes)*	**https://goo.gl/ DJ0siJ**
"This unit immerses fourth, fifth, and sixth grade students into several data analysis activities involving the deciphering of secret codes. Students will analyze the frequency of the letters of the alphabet [with pattern recognition] in a reading passage . . . and apply their findings to the solution of several transposition and substitution ciphers."	
https://www.nsa.gov/academia/_files/collected_learning/elementary/data_analysis/cipher_sleuths.pdf	

Lesson Plan: Divine Patterns

 This lesson plan is available for download at resources.corwin.com/ComputationalThinking.

Original Curriculum

CT Focus: Pattern Recognition	
Cross-Curricular Ties: Science	⬛ QR Code ⬛
Age Range: 8–16	https://goo.gl/123pNF
Duration: 30 minutes	
Scan the QR Code or type the URL to see a video example of how patterns can provide extra information.	

Overview

This lesson takes a deep look at patterns found in nature and challenges students to figure out which items are related to each other based on the patterns that they've found. Some items will be from the same family; others will have the same function. It's up to your students to figure out what the patterns are telling them!

Vocabulary

Pattern matching: Finding a theme that is repeated in more than one place.

Lesson Objectives

Students will be able to:

- Compare items to find similarities
- Infer information about items based on similarities
- Explain why they believe two items are related, based on patterns that they found

Materials and Resources

- Paper
- Pencils
- Whiteboard or projector
- Divine items to match

Preparation

1. Read the lesson and decide how it can best fit into the age range of students in your classroom.
2. Watch the video at https://goo.gl/123pNF in preparation of showing it to your class.
3. Gather pictures of "Divine Items." These will include a variety of images of things that have something in common. For example, find three or four images from three or four of the following groups:

    a. Animals mentioned in the video, with clear view of their slit pupils

    b. Carnivores with sharp teeth showing

    c. Animals with wings

    d. Foods with seeds showing (fruits)

    e. Green veggies

    f. Fish that glow (deep sea fish)

4. If students will be working in groups (Grades 3 and higher), print out enough "Divine Items" for each group. If the whole class is working together, you can cut items into individual cards for use with overhead projection.

5. Decide if you want to include the bits of "extra information" (e.g., "Carnivores") with the Divine Items. This is recommended with younger students. An alternative would be to have information sheets around the rooms that give clues about determining traits based on the patterns that you chose.

Activity

Step 1. Introduction—Show your class the video linked in step 2 of the Preparation list, and then ask:

- What feature did the animals in the video have in common? (Slit eyes)
- What behavior did the video tell us that all of those animals share? (They all hunt at night and are low to the ground.)
- If we found another animal that fit into that pattern (had slit eyes), what might we be able to conclude about it? (That it hunts at night and is low to the ground)

There are patterns all around us, and often, those patterns tell us things. Sometimes, we can determine extra information about one thing just because we recognize that it fits into a pattern with other things.

Step 2. Play with patterns—Have students group images appropriately to begin looking for patterns in the Divine Items. Challenge them to see how many groupings they can come up within 10 minutes. Have them write down both the patterns that they spotted and what they think it means so that they don't forget their thought process when it's time to share.

Keep in mind: Even though you started the exercise with items that go together in a certain way, never underestimate a group's ability to find new and valid patterns! The fact that they might come up with something other than what you planned doesn't mean that they're wrong!

Step 3. Share—After 10 minutes, ask students how many groupings they were able to make. Who thinks they came up with something that no one else found? Let each group share with the others at least two patterns and the corresponding information that the pattern related.

Step 4. Discuss together—Time to wrap up with a chat:

- What were the most interesting patterns that you found?
- Did you find any patterns that didn't seem to tell you anything?
- What was the largest grouping of patterns that you found? What did it tell you?
- Can you think of any other images that you wish had been included so that you could share your knowledge of what their patterns mean?

Step 5. In the real world—Computer scientists use pattern matching every day! To make computer programs as strong as they can be, programmers look for patterns in their problems and try to solve them based on solutions that they've used for other problems that were similar.

Some computer scientists called *data scientists* spend their days looking for patterns in information so that they can spot trends and failures in products and ideas.

Pattern matching is a key piece of problem solving. When you have a problem that seems really hard, you can often break it up into little pieces and look for patterns. These patterns just might point to a solution that will work for your bigger issue!

Solutions for first three sets (basic patterns)

1. Add 4 to the last number: 25

2. Add another level to the pyramid: 5 levels

3. Add another side to the polygon: an octagon

Solutions for second three sets (complex patterns)

4. Next decimal digit of pi: 5

5. Next binary representation (moving clockwise): both the top and right bubbles filled in.

6. Odds +4, Evens +1: a heptagon

9

Abstraction

When solving difficult problems, pattern recognition, or pattern matching, can be combined with skills like "abstraction" for greater effect. Sometimes, the most obvious pattern only indicates the very next item in a sequence (as with the Fibonacci series described in the previous chapter), but further analysis can lead to a solution that works all the way down the line.

Abstraction is the practice of ignoring certain details in order to come up with a solution that works for a more general problem. It can be a tough idea to grasp, but it's really just a way of letting go of details to make a process easier. In the real world, you could apply abstraction to the task of making a bed. You don't need to know exactly what pattern sheets you'll be using to tell someone how to make a bed properly. You don't even need to know the color of the blankets that go on top or how many pillows there will be. You can intentionally give directions that abstract out those details so that the bed maker can fill them in with the specifics when the need arises.

Abstraction example:

Here you see a flower with five petals, a flower with seven petals, and a flower with nine petals. Most of us would naturally abstract out the number of petals and just call them "flowers."

Parameter: An extra bit of information passed to an abstracted function that allows it to create something more specific.

It is possible, however, that we could add a **parameter** to the "flower" description so that we can get those petal-number details back later. For example: flower(5) is the flower with five petals, and flower(7) would be the flower with seven petals.

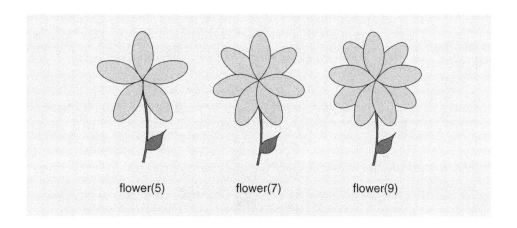

flower(5)   flower(7)   flower(9)

In the art of problem solving, abstraction can be a bit like pointing out the obvious. Let's take the final puzzle from the pattern matching section as an example (Figure 9.1).

FIGURE 9.1 Parameter of Sides, Visual

One abstracted instruction for any given item in the sequence of shapes could be "It is a shaded regular polygon, the same radius as the others, with some number of sides."

Simple but essential, yes? We're off to a good start.

Even more help would be to know exactly *how many* sides should be in any polygon in that series. Now, we know we're looking for a number. This is where we use pattern matching (Figure 9.2).

5   3   7   5   9 _____

FIGURE 9.2 Parameter of Sides, Numeric

Figure 9.2 shows that the only thing we have left to figure out for our abstracted instructions to work is the number of sides for each polygon.

Variable: A placeholder for a value that can change.

If we look at the numbers as their own series, we can compare them to their position in the list. We will use the **variable** n to represent the index of each number. The index is simply the specific location in the sequence (the first number in the sequence is $n = 1$, the second is $n = 2$, and so on.) To try to help the pattern along, we'll make a table (Table 9.1).

TABLE 9.1 Index to Number Value

N	VALUE	NOTES
1	5	$n + 4$
2	3	$n + 1$
3	7	$n + 4$
4	5	$n + 1$
5	9	$n + 4$

Without too much extra work, we are able to start seeing a pattern develop. It would appear that when n is odd, the polygon has $n + 4$ sides, and when n is even, it has only $n + 1$ sides. Now that we know the formula, we can plug our specific index into our abstracted algorithm and solve for any polygon in the series. Are you starting to see the efficiency of abstraction?

Abstraction Resources

Here are some example lessons, followed by an abstraction lesson called "So Abstract."

Abstraction by Code.org *(Age 7–12, approx. 45 minutes)*	
"We'll combine your students' everyday routine and a Mad Libs-style thinking game to help your class learn about the effectiveness of abstraction."	**https://goo.gl/ jakLsz**
https://studio.code.org/s/20-hour/stage/14/puzzle/1	

Plants by ISTE and CSTA *(Ages 5–10, approx. 45 minutes)*	
"Bring abstraction into a student's everyday life by highlighting the computational thinking (CT) concepts that they use in other subjects. In this lesson, students will read a story about a child who is dedicated to growing a garden. In summarizing that story, students will learn how abstracting out details makes an easier task of relating what they read."	**https://goo.gl/ d8ByLG**
https://csta.acm.org/Curriculum/sub/CurrFiles/472.11CTTeacherResources_ 2ed-SP-vF.pdf#page=18	

Red Black Mind Meld by Queen Mary University of London *(Ages 8 and older, approx. 30 minutes)*	
"Do a magic trick where you apparently control a person's actions through the power of thought. A prediction you make about the red and black cards turns out to be true even though no one saw the cards and the person freely picked them at random. You then use abstraction and logical thinking to prove the trick (which is self-working, so an algorithm) always works. You create a mathematical model of the cards and then use algebra to prove a property always holds—the same property that you made the prediction about."	**https://goo.gl/ 19QSzO**
https://teachinglondoncomputing.files.wordpress.com/2015/01/activity- redblackmindmeld.pdf	

This lesson plan is available for download at resources.corwin.com/ComputationalThinking.

Original Curriculum

CT Focus: Abstraction
Cross-Curricular Ties: English Language Arts
Age Range: 9–14
Duration: Approx. 30 minutes (more for older students)

Overview

In this activity, students will assume the role of a newspaper writer being sent out on assignment to cover special assignments for clients. To complete their articles, students will need to use abstraction to keep things simple and within the word count dictated by their editor.

Vocabulary

Abstraction: Getting rid of some of the details in a problem (forever or for just a little while).

Lesson Objectives

Students will be able to:

- Communicate with classmates to gather details that are important to their articles
- Determine whether information is important to include in their writing
- Demonstrate the concept of abstraction by leaving certain information out of their article
- Create a written piece that fits within the guidelines set by their editor

Materials and Resources

- Paper
- Pencils
- Whiteboard or projector
- Sample news articles

Preparation

1. Read the lesson and decide which model works best for your classroom:

    a. Young students—Children interview one another and put short stories (8–12 words) together in their heads for oral presentation.

    b. Middle elementary—Students write a short article with three abstractions, then share with the class. The finished piece should be 30–40 words.

    c. Upper elementary or middle school—Students work on two full-length articles that use the same template but demonstrate authentic representations of two different people. These should be 50–60 words each.

  2. Assign interviewees to students. It is okay to let students choose whom they are going to interview on the fly, but it can save some chaos to have pairs (or trios) planned in advance.

Activity

Step 1. Introduction—Let your class know that they have all been turned into roving reporters for *Computational Thinking Daily.* Each student will be given an assignment and expected to have it on the editor's desk by the appropriate deadline (this could be 30 minutes from the start of the activity or several days later, depending on the quality you expect of the finished product).

As editor-in-chief, you will be the reporters' new boss. You've decided to make some changes around here, and you're going to get this place operating as efficiently as possible. From now on, when reporters write features on other students, all of them must fit the same template and fit into the word count allotted for the daily paper.

Let students know that you have somehow lost the template, but you will show them two finished articles to see if they can help you create a new one.

Share with the class that you need them to use abstraction to find the details that they can ignore when creating the new template copy.

With your class, compare the two appropriate articles for your age group. Have them indicate what needs to be abstracted out by underlining the words. Those underlines will later become blank spaces where they can put their own details after they have completed their interviews.

Have students come up with questions (alone or as a class) that they can ask of their interviewees. Does it make sense to ask questions that we can't write about? Nope. Knowing which questions are relevant to the article and which questions you should ignore for this interview is another type of abstraction!

Step 2. Ink slinging—It's time for students to have their interviews! Allow students to use the questions they've created to find out more about their partner. Encourage older students to take notes to make remembering easier.

After a good amount of time has passed (you will need to judge for your class), ask students to conclude their interviews and head back to their seats to begin writing. If you are working with younger students, you'll likely want to have them stop where they are and stand up to share them immediately.

Have a copy of the blank template on the overhead projector for students to use in the creation of their articles. Allow them an appropriate amount of time to write, and remind them a few times to abstract out details to make sure that they hit their target word count.

Step 3. Share—When students are finished, encourage them to share their stories with the interviewees. Give students the chance to stand and read their articles to the rest of the class. Be sure to celebrate successes with applause.

Step 4. Discuss together—Ask your class about their experience with abstraction:

- Was it sometimes difficult to figure out what to abstract out when writing your article?
- Were there any ways that abstraction made this assignment easier?
- Can you think of other places that we abstract out information for just a little while (like we did when we made the template)?
  - o The "Name:" space on your assignment papers
  - o The "Day of the week" space on the board
  - o Pretty much anywhere that we save a place for something that changes
- Can you think of other places that we abstract out information for good, just to make things simple?
  - o Home address. You don't add "United States" or "Earth."
  - o Age. You don't tell people how many days and hours old you are.
  - o What you did last night. You don't include things like putting your clothes in the laundry, chewing your food, or going to the bathroom.

Step 5. In the real world—In computer science, abstraction is used in a couple of very different ways.

Programmers rarely think about abstracting out details. Usually, they do it naturally by finding a solution that works for one problem, and recognizing that it can also work for other problems if they change a couple of elements. The process of figuring out what those elements are is one form of abstraction. Yes, they ignore the details for a moment, but they understand that those details need to be fed back into the solution in order to get an answer. This is very similar to where we created blanks to save a place for the interviewee's name and eye color.

Data scientists use abstraction a little differently. Often, when they create a computer model of something like a flock of geese migrating, they determine that some details are just not necessary in creating a visual prediction. For example, they may feel like it's okay to have solid blue dots show the paths of the group of birds, instead of needing to have accurate images with beaks and flapping wings. Technically, this is also abstracting out details, but this time, the scientists have no intention of bringing the details back. This is similar to how we chose to leave some information out of our article, because it didn't fit into the subject of the template.

SAMPLE STORIES

Young Students

"This is Mehal. He has brown eyes."

"This is Juana. She has blue eyes."

Middle Elementary

"This article is about Tanya. She was born in February and loves puppies. Her favorite food is pizza, and she likes to eat it for breakfast. Tanya's favorite subject in school is math."

"This article is about Ryan. He was born in December and loves snow. His favorite food is broccoli with cheese, and he likes to eat it for every meal. Ryan's favorite subject in school is art."

Upper Elementary and Middle School

"This week, I got to interview Paula to learn a little more about her life and her collection of bells. Paula says that bells are interesting because they are pretty and they used to be very important in the old days. Paula is the only child in her family. She likes school, and her favorite subject is reading."

"This week, I got to interview JD to learn a little more about his life and his collection of books. JD says that books are interesting because they make you feel like you are in a whole different world. JD is the third child in his family. He likes cookies, and his favorite subject is recess."

10

Automation

By now, you've seen a few examples of automation, even if you weren't aware that the feature had a name. Any time there's an algorithm involved, there is some level of automation nearby. When you use automation, you're controlling a process (by automatic means) and reducing human intervention to a minimum. Generally, we think of automation as work being carried out by machine, but it could just as easily be the simplification of work for you or me.

All forms of mathematical functions are automations in a way. They are putting solutions in a form that can be followed by someone (or something) other than the original problem solver. It can also be the result of putting solutions into a form that works for multiple tasks. With the polygons from our chapter on pattern recognition, automation includes writing out our final algorithm for describing the nth shape in the series.

"It is a shaded regular polygon, the same radius as the others, with $n + 4$ sides when n is odd, and $n + 1$ sides when n is even."

To automate this further, we could create a computer program that asks us for n and returns the polygon for us. More automated still would be a program that simply output all of the polygons along with their n index so that no human intervention is required at all.

Obviously, automation is a double-edged sword. We don't want to get to the point where machines are doing all of the work and all of the thinking for us all of the time. Yet, many discoveries have only been possible through the help of automation. The largest prime number, for example, is 17 *million* digits long. Dividing it by a *single* one-digit number would take a scientist more than twenty-eight weeks by hand! Now imagine doing that for every possible prime factor (and there are literally trillions of them). Someone could spend their whole life doing nothing but long division.

There are practical applications for automation for our students, as well. Imagine them filling in the cells of a spreadsheet instantly with a formula instead of tediously doing so by hand. Even mail-merging party invitations or creating a music playlist would be examples of how automation could be useful for kids.

Have you ever used a flowchart?

Flowcharts (also known as *decision trees*) are used as a way of automating the decision-making process (Figure 10.1). They could be used either to visualize the steps that a machine might take when using an algorithm or to make a decision's outcome more obvious to a human.

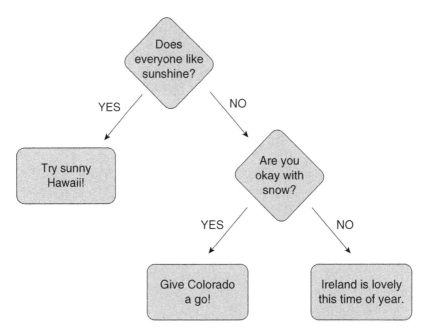

FIGURE 10.1 Flowchart for Deciding on a Location for Your Movie

Automation Resources

The lessons here can be scaled up or down but are suited best for the middle to high school crowd. Following these resources is a lesson plan called "Algorithms and Automation: A Compliment Generator."

Divide and Conquer by Queen Mary University of London *(Age 11 and older, approx. 45 minutes)*	
"In this lesson, students will use a 'divide-and-conquer' strategy to solve the mystery of 'stolen crystals' using decomposition to break the problem into smaller problems and algorithmic design (automation) to plan a solution strategy."	**https://goo.gl/ 5F5Pq9**
https://docs.google.com/document/d/1DMDuomVc5gZ_ NSaC3afERx40uESWweydMICqetin3to/edit	

Calculating Surface Area by Google Education *(Ages 12–16, approx. 45 minutes)*	https://goo.gl/ nOVZfB
"Use this program to apply students' knowledge of surface area formulas to automatically calculate the surface areas of several geometric objects: cube, rectangular prism, cylinder, sphere. Have students analyze, fill in parts of, or use the program to check results to exercises they are already working on. This program could be used to further your understanding of how you could use Python in the classroom, as a demonstration or discussion with your students, or as a way to introduce various computational thinking (CT) concepts, such as pattern recognition or abstraction, to your students by inviting them to extend the existing functionality of the program."	
https://docs.google.com/ document/d/1pDf7DHtGvmFkrPxg0EmY0HAMoQsCoLaYsu9ZQWmba7g/edit	

Sorting Algorithms by CS Unplugged *(Ages 12–16, approx. 45 minutes)*	http://goo.gl/ Oj06WO
"Almost any list that comes out of a computer is sorted into some sort of order, and there are many more sorted lists inside computers that the user doesn't see. Many clever algorithms have been devised for putting values into order efficiently. In this activity students compare different algorithms to sort weights in order."	
http://csunplugged.org/sorting-algorithms	

Lesson Plan: Algorithms and Automation—
A Compliment Generator

 This lesson plan is available for download at resources.corwin.com/ComputationalThinking.

Original Curriculum

CT Focus: Automation	
Cross-Curricular Ties: English and Language Arts	
Age Range: 10–16	https://goo.gl/ZfsbTD
Duration: 45 minutes	
Scan the QR Code or type the URL to see a teacher-facing YouTube video on algorithms.	

Overview

With this activity, students will learn about the relationship between algorithms and automation by creating a compliment generator. Students will figure out how to break sentences into chunks (beginning, middle, end) and then how to mix and match those chunks into new sentences. Once the procedure has been identified, students will write the algorithms for their generators, so that the procedure can be automated.

Vocabulary

Algorithm: A list of steps that can be followed to carry out a task.

Automation: Having a machine (such as a computer) do work for us, so that we don't have to do it ourselves.

Pseudocode: Instructions that look like they could be a computer program, but they are easier to read and don't necessarily follow rules of any specific programming language.

Lesson Objectives

Students will be able to:

- Break sentences apart into appropriate sections for randomization
- Compose sentences from random pieces
- Write an algorithm that explains the actions that the student's "machine" should take to automate the sentence-building procedure.

Materials and Resources

- Paper
- Pencils
- Whiteboard or projector
- Paper cups (three per group)

Preparation

1. Read the lesson and review the video linked with a QR code at the beginning of this lesson for better understanding of "algorithms" and "automation."

Activity

Step 1. Introduction—This lesson can do with a little prep around algorithms. Since algorithms and automation are so closely related (and both start with the letter *a*), it's easy to confuse the two.

First, have a chat about algorithms.

- Has anyone ever heard of an algorithm before?
  - What is it?
  - What do you think it might be?
- An algorithm is just a list of instructions that you can follow to finish a task. It's like a recipe or a step-by-step tutorial for modding your video game.
  - What else can you think of that might be an algorithm?

Now, take some time to come up with an algorithm for something students do every day, like getting ready for school or cleaning the kitchen.

Allow your class to come up with a couple more algorithms, until you're comfortable that they understand what an algorithm is. You might want to take the opportunity to let the students create one with a neighbor and share it with the class.

Algorithms let us prepare things for automation.

- Has anyone heard the term *automation* before?
  - What does *automation* mean to you?
  - Doing something automatically?
  - Having a machine do our work?
- Essentially it's having a machine or tool do work for us so that we don't have to do it ourselves. What do you use daily that automates things for you?
  - A calculator
  - A car
  - A printer
- What does it automate, do you suppose?

Step 2. Program and run—Once you've gone through that thought exercise, you're ready to get your students thinking about setting a task up to be automated. Let them know that they will be gathering into small groups to prepare a task for automation. One person will be the "machine," and everyone else will be part of the programming team. (If you have very young students, you will likely want to have the whole class program while you act as the machine.)

Now, time for the activity!

Share some compliments with your class that fit the same structure as these:

"You are a beautiful person."

"He is a kind human being."

"She is a strong role model."

You can deliver these authentically to your students, but be sure to write them down on the board or overhead screen so that you can dissect them later.

- What did all of those compliments have in common? (The structure)
- What if we wanted to mix these up?
    - "You are a kind role model."
    - "He is a strong person."
    - "She is a beautiful human being."
- Where can we break these sentences up to be able to mix them all around?
    - "You are"
    - "He is"
    - "She is"
    - "a kind"
    - "a strong"
    - "a beautiful"
    - "role model"
    - "person."
    - "human being."
- Where should the subject (alternatively, pronoun) be?
- Where should the predicate (alternatively, verb) be?
- How about the adverbs and adjectives?

- What other patterns do you see?
- Can we add some other chunks to swap in?
    - "That was"
    - "This can be"
    - "one sweet"
    - "the perfect"
    - "classmate."
    - "work of art."
- Let's choose some at random and see what we come up with!
    - "That was the perfect human being."
    - "She is one sweet classmate."

Now that your class sees where this is going, it's time for them to get in their groups to think about how this works. Give them these activity steps:

1. Create 6–10 phrases that fit the template above.
2. Cut the phrases into individual strips, then cut the strips into three appropriate chunks for mixing.
3. Label one cup "Beginnings" and put all the chunks of sentence beginnings in that cup. Do the same for "Middles" and "Ends."
4. Create an algorithm for your "compliment generator machine" (CGM) using pseudocode.
    a. What steps will your CGM need to follow in order to generate a new compliment each time you run it?
    b. How specific do you need to be to make sure your program runs without any errors?
    c. Don't forget to include steps for what to do with the papers after the compliment has been delivered.
5. Program the CGM by reading it your algorithm.
6. Run the CGM to see if it had the desired result.
7. If there was a problem (bug), fix your algorithm, then program and run the CGM again.

Step 3. Share—When students have finished their generators, allow each group to run their generator for the class. Did every CGM work the same?

Step 4. Discuss together—Gather the students together to talk about their experience.

- What was the hardest part of automating this task?
- Did you get the chance to look for issues with your algorithm and fix it for a better automation?
- Can you think of other tasks that you could create an algorithm for?
- What do you think the relationship is between algorithms and automation?

Step 5. In the real world—Algorithms are without a doubt the most important part of automating, and automation is the single largest motivation for developing computer programs. Computer scientists wouldn't even be necessary if we didn't need to automate.

More than 4,000 years ago, mathematicians were already trying to automate complex calculations using the abacus. From that point, calculators (and soon computers) became more and more intelligent. Now, they are able to automate tasks like finding unbelievably large prime numbers or sequencing the human genome—jobs that just couldn't be done by hand.

Behind every computer automation there is a computer program, and behind every computer program, there is an algorithm.

A LAST WORD ON COMPUTATIONAL THINKING

Automation is helpful, but without the other elements of CT, it can be elusive. Used together, decomposition, pattern recognition, abstraction, and automation are powerful tools to knock down the walls of the unknown. The best part is that you can start using these skills in your classes immediately. Challenge your students to tear big problems down into pieces. Ask them to look at those pieces for similarities with problems that they've already solved. See if they can put into words the things they know, while abstracting out the details that have them stumped. They may or may not come out the other side with an algorithm for automation, but they will end up with a method for tackling challenges that could have otherwise left them stumped and frustrated.

WHAT'S NEXT?

You now know more than most educators do about computational thinking. We hope you draw parallels between CT and everyday learning activities within the subjects or grades you teach.

Get ready for a trip into another aspect of thinking that may hold the key to success in STEM and computer science—spatial reasoning. We'll consider how spatial reasoning can be a natural feature of the learning environment, and then, in the next chapter, consider how "making" takes kids imaginations and skills to the big screen!

11

Activities That Foster Spatial Reasoning

Before he was two years old, future Massachusetts Institute of Technology (MIT) computer scientist, mathematician, and educator Seymour Papert (whom we introduced in Chapter 2) became fascinated with gears. Playing with gears was his favorite pastime, and several years on, little Seymour's first project with an Erector Set was a simple gear system. As he notes in the preface to *Mindstorms: Children, Computers, and Powerful Ideas*, "I became adept at turning wheels in my head and at making chains of cause and effect. I found particular pleasure in such systems as the differential gear, which does not follow a simple linear chain of causality" (Papert, 1980, p. xviii). His ability to imagine gears and the ways the differential gear distributes motion influenced what he deemed his most significant mathematical development during elementary school. "Gears, serving as models, carried many otherwise abstract ideas into my head. I clearly remember two examples from school math. I saw multiplication tables as gears, and my first brush with equations in two variables (e.g., $3x + 4y = 10$) immediately evoked the differential. By the time I had made a mental gear model of the relation between x and y, figuring how many teeth each gear needed, the equation had become a comfortable friend" (pp. xviii–xix).

Papert fits with many who are at the top of their game in science, technology, engineering, and mathematics (STEM) fields. Multiple studies show thinkers like Papert exhibit strong **spatial reasoning** abilities (Wai, Lubinski, & Benbow, 2009). They are, as Papert's story illustrates, able to generate visual images and even make sense of abstract concepts by associating them with mental models. We'll dig into spatial reasoning a bit soon, because this ability is integral to STEM and, particularly, to computer science (CS). Afterward, we'll talk about everyday (and non-CS) activities that can boost spatial reasoning.

> **Spatial reasoning**: The ability to generate, retain, retrieve, and transform well-structured visual images.

Before we leave Papert's story, though, let's think about the "fascination factor." Papert loved gears and felt happy when he played with or even just thought about gears. Without that spark of fascination, could his imagination have otherwise been unleashed? Without deep interest, could he have sustained the mental effort it took to figure out how gears operate as a system? Or stuck with it long enough to begin automatically associating other phenomena, such as number relationships in multiplication, to the ways gears function? A sheer love for gears carried his thinking a long way. As you support students in their construction of new meaning, be attuned to the unique "fascination factor" that lights a fire in each of them.

SPATIAL ABILITIES TIED TO SUCCESS IN STEM

What do we mean by spatial reasoning? Generally, spatial reasoning is the ability to generate, retain, retrieve, and transform well-structured visual images (Wai et al., 2009).

To develop this idea a bit, spatial reasoning involves visualizing two- and three-dimensional (2D and 3D) forms, being able to mentally rotate them in space, and also imagine cross-sections and inner dimensions. There's a dynamic aspect, too, as with Papert's gears story, of being able to predict how objects move and how different forms interact mechanically.

Spatial reasoning is associated with the ability to think about abstract and complex ideas. In fact, a tiny area of the brain called the *intraparietal sulcus* processes both visual representation of numbers in children and higher order math reasoning in adults (N. Newcombe & L. Jones, personal communication, December 4, 2015).

The tasks in Figure 11.1 get at spatial reasoning ability (Wai et al., 2009). One choice corresponds with each figure. Can you solve them? Can your students? (Correct answers can be found at the end of this chapter.)

It turns out spatial reasoning is integral to problem posing and problem solving in STEM (Wai et al., 2009). Think about the spatial nature of architecture, video game development, modeling DNA, and forces operating on structures in engineering. Imagine surgery—from interpreting the X-ray or MRI to doing the cutting. All kinds of careers require being able to move from 2D to 3D and back, and being able to visualize and rotate. Even movie-making requires a director to be able to think about action in an environment that has yet to be made physical.

Not surprisingly, spatial ability has been shown to be a predictor of participation in both the arts and STEM occupations (Wai et al., 2009). For those less spatial, the confidence to try new things can go a long way toward strengthening spatial thinking. And with awareness of its importance, teachers can convey to their students how useful and enjoyable it can be to build things, to sketch, or to present information using graphical representations.

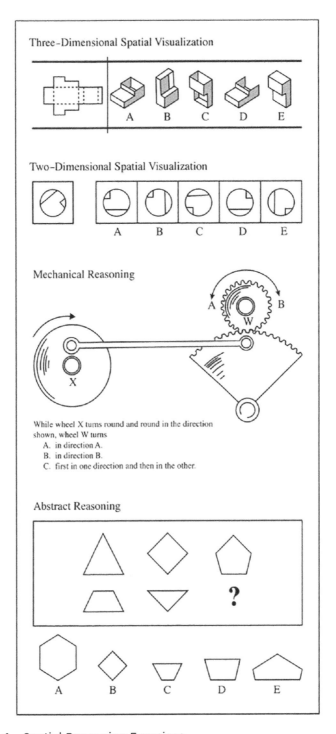

FIGURE 11.1 Spatial Reasoning Exercises

Source: Wai, J., Lubinski, D., & Benbow, C. (2009)

Because computing mostly operates independently of the concrete world, the ability to think spatially is necessary for representing ideas as code, creating graphical representations, and modeling concepts. For a straightforward example, think of the simple games that beginning coders might learn to create in the programming language Python, such as a skiing game. A coder must understand the downward movements of the skier, the downward flow of the screen, and the shifting of the trees as she builds the game. Another example that is familiar to many is the changing of screens in games such as Super Mario. Coders must be able to visualize the layers of the game and structure the placement of the barriers as they develop the code.

Let's back up a bit and think about how spatial skills develop through life experience, play, and formal learning. Think about how you, a fully evolved adult, draw on spatial reasoning in these everyday activities:

- Interpreting a diagram to put an IKEA bed frame together
- Packing as many objects as can fit into a box for shipping
- Orienting yourself in a large and unfamiliar building, such as a hospital
- Skating to where the hockey puck is headed, not where it is at the moment
- Deciphering a map or blueprint
- Following a crochet or knitting pattern
- Designing a 3D world in Minecraft
- Understanding the layout of fictitious shires in Lord of the Rings

How do you feel about activities like these? Would you rather delegate them to others, or do you feel confident joy when tackling spatial tasks? Your answer may hinge on your earliest childhood experiences.

We start processing spatial information when our visual system matures at about three months. If you've seen a toddler's toy bin you know that spatial skills and hand-eye coordination develop together as young children play with toys like these:

- Worker bench and hammer with different shapes to pound
- Nesting boxes and stacking rings
- Toys with gears
- Chunky jigsaw puzzles

No definitive reason has been isolated to explain it, but as a group, boys outperform girls on tests of spatial ability. We don't know whether this is due to socialization, cultural expectations around play (Fromberg & Bergen, 2006), or some inherent gender difference. Not surprisingly, *all* children who have a rich play life become more adept spatially than those who have little to play with.

This difference matters when it comes to preparation for STEM. Children who have strong spatial relations are more ready when introduced to STEM subjects that require abstraction. One of the first places in school when this might matter significantly is in the shift from arithmetic to algebra ("Foundations for Success," 2008). Arithmetic is about computation of specific numbers. Algebra is about what is true in general for all whole numbers and integers. In its most general form, algebra is the study of mathematical symbols and the rules for manipulating these symbols. It is a unifying thread of almost all higher mathematics, and mathematics is the language of science. Because it is symbolic, it's abstract, and it is at the point when math changes from concrete to abstract that a lot us of decide we aren't math people. That's a shame because if we give students a pass when they say they don't want to pursue math, we've essentially helped shut the door to STEM academic and career options that should remain open as long as possible.

You should be wondering by now, "If spatial reasoning is important to STEM, how can I ensure students' spatial abilities are developing?" The good news is *many* school activities build spatial ability. With a little attention, you can extend and reinforce them.

"SPATIALIZE" YOUR TEACHING

You can help students develop their spatial skills with minor intervention. Increase students' readiness to manage abstraction in math and computer science by taking Nora Newcombe's advice and "spatialize" your teaching (Newcombe, 2010). Here are some ideas for helping students develop spatial visualizations for discovery and communication.

Classroom enrichment. Hands-on learning stations are de rigueur in primary classrooms and have a place in classrooms for older students, too. Offer a revolving assortment of activities in your stations with tangram, puzzle, and take-it-apart stations; K'NEX, erector set, and other building stations; and spatial and acuity games like Battleship, Jenga, Tetris, and Angry Birds. Another game that draws on and develops spatial relations is chess. Imagining not just the moves available on the board now but three turns ahead is a feat of visualization.

Be alert to opportunities to enrich your curriculum, too. Add a knot-tying station during an oceans project and a quilt-piecing station during studies of pioneer life. An origami (paper-folding) station would be perfectly suited to geometry.

Teach toward visual literacy. Teach students to interpret many types of diagrams, graphs, infographics, and other visual representations. Visual literacy improves with direct instruction; your first exposure to the periodic table of the elements was probably accompanied by a teacher's explanation. Repeated practice matters, too. It likely took repeated study of the periodic table before you appreciated the beautiful organization and depth of information presented there.

Model spatial reasoning. Think aloud and use vocabulary related to form, position, direction, size, and scale. Use your hands, too. Gesturing is shown to aid spatial understanding and communication (Ehrlich, Levine, & Goldin-Meadow, 2006).

Sketch. Many breakthroughs were fleshed out with "back of the napkin" sketches, and with practice, putting thinking to paper will become second nature to your students. Sketch as you teach and encourage students to sketch. Teach them to represent systems and causal relationships with diagrams, storyboards, and flowcharts. Don't let students get hung up on a perceived lack of artistic skill. Say, "We aren't drawing here, we're sketching, just putting ideas down on paper so we can talk about them."

WRAPPING IT UP

Are you beginning to see the affordances of "spatializing" your teaching? Consider next the possibilities of building your students abilities through the *very* spatial hands-on and minds-on activities inherent in the maker movement that is taking schools by storm.

Here are the answers to the spatial puzzles on page 86, Figure 11.1: A, A, C, D.

12

Making With Code

Over the past few years, *making* has become a buzzword, a practice, and a passion in schools intent on providing authentic, student-driven, and hands-on learning experiences. Making is to a degree an offshoot of the home shop, with do-it-yourself invention, fabrication, and repair involving woodworking, electronics, and the like. But making goes beyond that in at least two ways. First, it's communal. People no longer toil alone in the garage but meet in a common space, a *makerspace,* to share tools, ideas, and labor. (Why have a lathe when you use it once a year? Where better to learn to operate a lathe than in a place where people skilled with lathes are apt to meet?) The second reason takes us from the 20th-century "Popular Mechanics" era right into this digital age. Makerspaces are also a place for physical computing, that is, robotics, e-textiles, three-dimensional (3D) printing, and other projects that involve programming.

Maker movement: A trend in which people gather in a shared workspace equipped for the invention and fabrication of unique products.

Teachers on the lookout for the new opportunities for "hands on, minds on" learning have seen what goes on in community makerspaces and are joining the **maker movement** with their students. They see how a makerspace is the perfect environment for students to develop inventive thinking, spatial reasoning, motor skills, and programming chops. Enter, maker education!

Follow the Twitter hashtag #makerED and meet educators enthusiastic about making.

The time is right for making. And, with the advent of low-cost and open-source programmable microprocessors, inexpensive electronics components, and new fabrication tools, it's also a great way to learn to code.

Making doesn't always involve computers, but given the intentions of this book, we focus here on experiences that involve programming. Here are just a few of the inventions students are making with code.

- *Musical fruit.* Third-grade makers create a working piano, attaching their MaKey MaKey,* a printed circuit board with a microcontroller, with alligator clips to parsnips (white keys) and carrots (black keys).

- *May the lights be with you.* Sixth graders program a Raspberry Pi,* a low-cost, credit card–sized computer, in the Python language to sync holiday light patterns with the Star Wars theme.

- *3D-printed stacking candles.* Middle school students use Tinkercad* to design 3D-printed molds for candles shaped like Lego. (They actually stack!)

- *Foam core farm.* Middle and elementary students work together to create jointed farm animals from foam board, then make their creatures move with programmable Hummingbird Robotics.*

- *Mopbot.* High school students are challenged to solve a kindergarten teacher's problem—water spills on the classroom floor. They invent Mopbot, a motion-sensing robotic mop made from Lego Mindstorms,* and frame it inside a cute laser-cut turtle with a 3D-printed handle.

Exciting stuff, yes? If you are beginning to imagine your students inventing with code, you are in good company. During the past few International Society for Technology in Education (ISTE) conferences (the biggest edtech gathering in the United States), attendees packed into standing-room-only sessions on making. However, unbridled enthusiasm for making could be a hopeful or worrisome sign. Making in schools has the potential to be a game-changer, a vehicle for creative, personalized, and hands-on learning that students might not otherwise be afforded in school (let alone outside of school). Making could also be the "flavor of the week," an expensive investment that dies on the vine when initial enthusiasm wanes. How can we both fulfill the promise and mitigate the hazards associated with making in school? Fortunately, some thoughtful practices are emerging.

First of all, making isn't about *stuff*. It's not even about the *space*. More than anything, making is *culture* and *design thinking*. If you are serious about making, do your homework. Join your school colleagues and engage in shared reading of Sylvia Martinez and Gary Stager's *Invent to Learn: Making, Tinkering, and Engineering in the Classroom* (2013). Read this "MakerEd bible" together to understand the constructionist philosophy and pedagogy behind making. Learn about design thinking and come away inspired by tales of invention. Once your team is on the same page, you can make decisions about incorporating meaningful making in your school. If you continue down the path toward making, pick up the free digital guide *Makerspace Playbook* (2013), a handbook full of checklists, safety tips, and sample projects.

MAKING WITHIN STEAM STUDIES

As you plan toward making, there are two complementary approaches we hope you will consider: (1) making as a way to address the school science, technology, engineering, arts, and math (STEAM) curricula, and (2) making as a freestyle opportunity for students to invent with few limits. With deliberate intention, you can have both.

When making is situated in STEAM, it brings these subjects to life. With a wealth of making materials and tools at your students' disposal, you will be more inclined to open up your curriculum to student-centered, inquiry-based approaches.

> Worth noting: Students whose teachers conduct hands-on learning activities on a weekly basis outperform their peers by more than 70 percent of a grade level in math and 40 percent of a grade level in science (Wenglinsky, 2000).

Take a page from educator Jackie Gerstein's playbook, whose integrated project *From Puppets to Robots* addresses, to different degrees, all of STEAM and other important learning dispositions (Gerstein, 2013). With a launch pad project like *From Puppets to Robots*, students learn design thinking and maker skills that help them get ready for more "freestyle" making later on.

> **"***The educator should be a tour guide of learning possibilities. Show learners the possibilities and then get out of their way.***"**
>
> —Jackie Gerstein, teacher and blogger

From Puppets to Robots begins with students exploring the history of puppetry and constructing shadow puppets and marionettes. Next comes an investigation of human movements and how movement can be incorporated into puppet design. In later lessons, students apply what they've learned to build robots that are intended to have a positive impact on humankind. Students experience STEAM in an immersive way as they:

- Explore the biomechanics of movement; experiment with force and motion relating to fulcrums and weight loads (Science)

- Investigate robotics through online simulations; learn AutoCAD design and programming to bring a robotic arm to life (Technology)

- Prototype and build a 3D self-standing robotic arm that can pick up objects (Engineering)

- Create shadow puppets; draw 2D robot patterns to translate to 3D using web-based design software; storyboard shadow puppet action for a play; write scripts and practice playacting (Arts)

- Measure for angle, size, and shape to draw, cut, and build prototypes (Mathematics)

And along the way, students:

- Experience design thinking and practice new strategies for solving complex problems

- Learn to use tools and basic construction techniques

- Learn safety practices necessary for "freestyle" access to the makerspace

- Work iteratively toward presentation-quality work

- Present both oral and written ideas effectively

- Practice teamwork and project management

Some people worry about making becoming too teacher-directed (there *are* a lot of cookie cutter projects out there!), but the beauty of a project like this is it's a scaffolded yet open-ended experience. Students are guided through design thinking processes and learn to use maker tools, with lots of room for personal inventiveness and creative expression.

DESIGN FOR DESIGN THINKING

Design thinking is an approach to problem solving closely aligned with the computational reasoning we promote in this book. Imagine your students designing a computer program or phone app, or entering into a makerspace with the mindset that they aren't dabbling, but, with their inventiveness, they are changing the world. With some exposure to design thinking, they *will* change the world.

Design thinking is problem solving fueled by empathy and observation. It's having your radar up to recognize how the world can be better, and taking action toward a solution. Design isn't necessarily a sequence of steps, but it is an iterative process that takes you from *think* to *thing*. There are many educational resources in the design thinking space, particularly since making came to school. We don't have room in this book to introduce them all, but we can help you get started. One approach to the design process we like a lot comes from the K12 Lab at the Stanford "D" (design) School (see Figure 12.1). This is an approach that causes students to think, see, feel, question, dither, prototype, trial, test, and modify their inventions in an iterative way. Consider these stages, always imagining the person (or animal, or environmental niche for that matter) who might be affected by the problem *and* the solution.

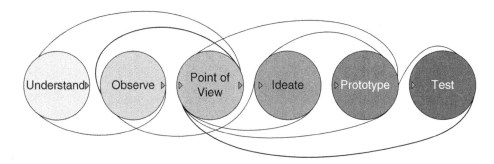

FIGURE 12.1   Design Processes From the K12 Lab, Stanford "D" School

Source: Stanford d.school K!2 Lab Wiki (https://dschool.stanford.edu/groups/k12/wiki/aedde/The_Design_Thinking_Process.html)

Here's more on each stage. Remember, these processes are suited to coding, making, and any other type of inventive thinking.

> *UNDERSTAND. Understanding is the first phase of the design thinking process. During this phase, students immerse themselves in learning. They talk to experts and conduct research. The goal is to develop empathy and background knowledge through these experiences. They use their developing understandings as a springboard as they begin to address design challenges.*

> *OBSERVE. Students become keen people watchers in the observation phase of the design thinking process. They watch how people behave and interact and they observe physical spaces and places. They talk to people about what they are doing, ask questions, and reflect on what they see. The understanding and observation phases of design thinking help students develop a sense of empathy.*

> *DEFINE. In this phase of design thinking, the focus is on becoming aware of people's needs and developing insights. The phrase "How might we . . ." is often used to define a point of view, which is a statement of the user + need + insight. This statement ends with a suggestion about how to make changes that will have an impact on people's experiences.*

> *IDEATE. Ideating is a critical component of design thinking. Students are challenged to brainstorm a myriad of ideas and to suspend judgment. No idea is too far-fetched and no one's ideas are rejected. Ideating is all about creativity and fun. In the ideation phase, quantity is encouraged. Students may be asked to generate a hundred ideas in a single session. They become silly, savvy, risk takers, wishful thinkers, and dreamers of the impossible . . . and the possible.*

PROTOTYPE. Prototyping is a rough and rapid portion of the design process. A prototype can be a sketch, model, or a cardboard box. It is a way to convey an idea quickly. Students learn that it is better to fail early and often as they create prototypes.

TEST. Testing is part of an iterative process that provides students with feedback. The purpose of testing is to learn what works and what doesn't, and then iterate. This means going back to your prototype and modifying it based on feedback. Testing ensures that students learn what works and what doesn't work for their users.

("Steps in a Design Thinking Process," 2009).

Moving from more structured making experiences (such as *From Puppets to Robots*, mentioned earlier) and freestyle making may call for in-between experiences. The big thinkers at IDEO, a design and innovation firm, and the Stanford D School have teamed up to bring design thinking to school. You will find many design projects and challenges, many suited to making, in the K12 Lab Network wiki: https://dschool.stanford.edu/groups/k12.

Give kids a chance to flex their design thinking muscles with exercises and design challenges such as these, also available at the K12 Lab Network:

- Five Chairs Exercise—Design and create five chairs for a single user.
- Marshmallow Challenge—Build towers with only spaghetti, marshmallows, tape, and string.
- Wallet Project—Design a wallet based on a partner's unique preferences.
- The Hamster Challenge—Design habitats that make life better for pet hamsters.
- Ramen Project—Design and rapidly prototype a better ramen eating experience.
- Car Maintenance Redesign—Redesign the car maintenance experience.

Now: Challenge yourself! You are steeped in computational thinking now. What kind of computing solution might your students apply to the challenges in this list? How about the last one? How might students code their way to a better car maintenance experience?

"FREESTYLE" MAKING

Let's wrap up this trip into making and design thinking with a quick word about "freestyle" making. Ultimately, the goal of education is to maximize human potential, right? Let's think of our students not just as learners but as *inventors*, and get out of their way! Imagine gradually letting go, moving from structured experiences to open access to the tools of invention.

When they sit down with programmable devices or enter the makerspace equipped with skills and approaches to problem solving you've nurtured, kids will blow the doors off your—and their own—expectations of what they can do.

Open-ended, passion-driven making calls for flexible access to the instruments of invention. Making takes time. Consider how your school might allow for computer programming or making during lunch time, before or after school, or even evenings and weekends. (Some schools have turned their makerspaces into a community hub for making, inviting people of all ages to teach, learn, and make together.)

Another option is to hold **"genius hours"** as suggested by education leader Angela Maiers and adopted by thousands of teachers. Maiers (Maiers & Sandvold, 2014) asks an essential question that you might ask yourself:

Genius hours: Dedicated class time for students to explore their own passions.

What would happen if students were given the time, resources, and opportunity to pursue what they are most passionate about? She goes on to wonder, *How would this impact student engagement and students' perception of school?*

How profound to imagine students thinking of school as the place where their ideas take flight, where they invent with code, and where they put their hands to making real, tangible products of their imagination!

We'd like to end on a note of caution. Unless all kids have introductory experiences in coding and making, some will come to the opportunity more prepared than others. Those more ready will naturally inhabit the spaces where these things happen. Don't let one group of kids dominate the majority of resources and inventive learning spaces. The last thing you want is for kids to think that only some of us (and not others) are suited to coding and making. Strive for representative participation in your makerspaces and after-school coding clubs. You might have to take an extra step and invite kids in. Remember, those who create our technologies should be like those who use it. Your school environment is the first place where diversity of thought can be expressed for the benefit of the entire school community. Empower every potential coder and maker to make a difference in the world, and celebrate their contributions.

Part 4

Your Feature Presentation

You've accepted a part, gone through rehearsal, and now it's time to get this motion picture out to the masses! Your script might not be set, but the following chapters will help you to capture the essence of your role on the computer science stage. Places, everyone!

13

Designing a Curriculum Continuum Across K–12

Even in 2010, it would have been hard to imagine that America would be willing to adopt computer science (CS) classes in school at a large scale down to an elementary level. Of course, at the time, most of the CS curriculum out there was directed at college students and a few brave high schoolers.

In 2011, Thinkersmith began to shake up the status quo by introducing lessons that explored concepts like binary, functions, and even finite state automaton using art, crafting, and games to students as young as five or six. These activities allowed for a more basic treatment of subjects that had been previously deemed too lofty for kids and brought the fundamentals within reach of our youngest students.

In late 2013, Thinkersmith paired up with the newly formed Code.org on a project that was intended to provide a medium for students in K–8 to have their very first programming experience during a time period dubbed "CSEd Week" that happens each year, the second week in December. The Code.org experience, currently known as the Hour of Code™, launched a free curriculum, which included a combination of **unplugged** and online activities. It was instantly adopted by so many teachers as a long-term classroom experience that the duo decided to go back to the drawing board to create multiple options for different age groups. By autumn 2014, Code.org had released the first three courses in CS Fundamentals, blending online tutorials with unplugged lessons to walk students through the most important concepts in programming.

> **Unplugged**:
> Computer science learning activity not requiring a computer.

Although this was one of the first projects to make an entire CS curriculum accessible in elementary school without the need for technology, it was *not* the first programming environment targeted at children. In fact, Scratch* (https://scratch.mit.edu) from the Massachusetts Institute of Technology (MIT) had been around since March 2007. Scratch had already been widely adopted among middle school and after-school clubs, as well as forward thinking elementary classrooms.

Even prior to Scratch, Tim Bell and his crew in the CS Education Research Group at the University of Canterbury in New Zealand in 1998 released their original computer science activity book called *CS Unplugged*. These offline activities, intended to act as innovative supplements to a traditional curriculum, served as proof of the concept that computer science education could be both playful and effective at the same time.

By CSEd Week in 2015, the number of coding sites, apps, and tutorials on the market skyrocketed to include more than 100 hour-long experiences and nearly 20 environments for use in elementary education ("Cool Coding Apps and Websites for Kids," n.d.). What's even better is that the love of CS has spread and the public is finally starting to understand how crucial the subject is to today's students.

Many countries are getting on board. In 2013, the United Kingdom announced its intention to bring CS to its elementary schools. Estonia, Finland, and Italy were close behind (Pretz, 2014). Here in the states, official CS announcements have been made in New York City and all of Arkansas, with several more states ready to pounce . . . as soon as they wrap their heads around what a K–12 pathway might look like.

Some wrongfully imagine that introducing CS to students in elementary school means sitting kindergartners behind a screen and asking them to debug programs for hours on end. Others believe that their district already teaches CS because they have classes dedicated to keyboarding, word processing, or graphic design. We'll address each of those assumptions individually, starting with the latter.

The truth is, many people don't know the difference between computer science and computer literacy (*Images of Computer Science*, 2015). The assumption is that if students know how to use a computer, they will have a complete skill set for graduation. In reality, knowing how to use a computer will be as necessary to the class of 2020 as knowing how to read, while understanding basic CS (think: algorithms, debugging, and simple coding skills) will compare to understanding arithmetic.

Function: A piece of code that you can call over and over again.

Conditional: Block of code that can only run under certain conditions.

Just as there are age-appropriate first steps in every other subject, there are good starting places for young students to learn CS. Let's start with language. Words like **function** and **conditional** are not typical of a kindergartner's vocabulary.

Fortunately, those are just words concealing some very manageable ideas. With the language of CS, as with history or any other science, repeated exposure in multiple contexts allows the language of the discipline to become more natural.

Many of the most foundational CS concepts can be taught with strategic analog activities. Want to learn about **loops**? Do a dance. Want to teach functions? Explore the structure of a song with a repeating chorus. Trying to figure out how to explain sequence or debugging? Write simple instructions on slips of paper and have groups organize them and act them out to see if they create the desired result. Computer science is a simulation of life; keep this in mind as you challenge yourself to convert code into real-life activities.

> **Loop**: A set of instructions to be repeated until a condition is met.

At the moment, computer science education is tricky because we can't count on students to come into any one grade with a predictable CS history. This can lead to undifferentiated teaching approaches that fall short of the mark when every student is treated as a beginner, no matter how experienced he or she might be. In an ideal world, students would be exposed to computer science all along the K–12 pathway, with teachers keeping an appropriate end-goal in mind for each grade.

14

Important Ideas Across All Grades

Fortunately, because computer science (CS) is still not required in schools, there is no pressure to make sure every single idea sticks and that students come away reciting definitions for every CS term. Instead, focus on making the experience useful, fun, and encouraging. Imagine the exposure you give students now gets them ready and enthused for meaningful experiences ahead.

No matter the age of students or how they're being exposed to CS, poor CS instruction is worse than no computer science at all. Here are some tips to ensure that the learning experiences you offer are productive and life-changing for your students.

PAIR PROGRAMMING

We have mentioned this a couple of times now, but just in case you're only skimming through the sections that pertain to you, we'll talk about pair programming a bit more. It's that important!

In pair programming two students sit at the same computer. One is the driver (moving the mouse and typing at the keyboard) while the other is the navigator (reading through the problem and keeping an eye on the big picture). When working as a duo, students will feel inclined to talk through problems out loud, often inspiring solutions where otherwise progress would be halted. Pair programming has a nice effect once a class gets to text-based coding, too, in that students are more likely to follow conventions (like proper formatting and commenting) when someone is constantly watching over their shoulder!

LEARNING TO LEARN

Computer science education is more about learning to learn than it is about anything else. Unlike in mathematics, reading, or writing, the entire landscape of CS will change several times over between the time students begin kindergarten and when they graduate from high school. Students need to be prepared for this and be ready to adapt as quickly as the technologies around them do.

This subject does not lend itself to rote learning. To be a true computer scientist, you must be able to think through an issue, break it apart, find a solution, and then figure out how that solution might be used in other ways. As such, it doesn't make sense to learn CS only through classroom lecture followed by practice on a teaching example. Effective CS education should include plenty of planning, experimentation, and room for revision. Some might label this "inquiry-based learning," and we wouldn't argue. It's also a form of the scientific method and creative problem solving. Whatever you call it, if an instructor swoops in to save a student from failure, they're robbing students of half of their learning opportunity.

There is a better way to deal with failure in CS than to rescue someone from it. One of the most helpful techniques is to acknowledge discomfort and encourage persistence. Let students know that CS is always going to be there and that it is their friend. Failure is not the end point in programming. Failure is a clue to help you make your code better. While failure and frustration go hand in hand, neither has to be a negative thing when it comes to CS. Failure is an indicator of new paths, and frustration is a sign that you're working through something difficult—both lead to amazing educational opportunities, as long as students learn to welcome them instead of fear them.

RESOURCES AT THE READY

In this age of ubiquitous multimedia and omnipresent mobile devices, teachers often feel like they're waging an uphill battle. Computer science gives teachers the opportunity to stop suppressing student interests and start incorporating them into their lessons.

Very little of CS is routine memorization. It is much more important that students internalize the "how" aspect of coding. Take away some of the anxiety around CS by maintaining a list of resources that persist through every assignment. For example, try having a class web page full of links where students can travel at any time, during any assignment. Allow students to use their phones to browse for solutions while they're coding on the school computer. Even if they find the exact answer they're looking for, they'll still have to enter the solution onto the computer on their own, strengthening their understanding of "what goes where and why."

For older learners, consider a class collaboration site, like Piazza* (www .piazza.com), where students can communicate with one another, asking questions and providing answers digitally. At a K–5 level, have optional printouts with strategic tips and hints that you place in a stack at the front of the room (without any fanfare). Students will learn to see that piece of paper as a gift.

Most importantly, let students use one another. It makes no sense to make collaboration off limits in CS education. Feel free to lay ground rules if it makes you feel more comfortable. Some examples might be:

- Only pencil/paper communication is allowed

- You cannot provide answers directly; instead, ask leading questions

- The helper must stand by the computer of the helpee

While those suggestions should be effective in helping students not to cheat outright, students tend to get protective enough over their code that extra rules aren't usually necessary.

One final tip on the resources front. Collaboration can sometimes be confusing and noisy. Consider having nonverbal cues to indicate a pair's comfort at any given moment. One popular trick is to have a stack of colored cups or sticky notes to go over the corner of the monitor that signal status:

- Nothing—Rockin' and rollin' on my own

- Green—Feeling confident and willing to help others

- Yellow—Feeling challenged and could use a peer to bounce things off of

- Red—Have already consulted peers and now need teacher help

Not only does a system like this cut down on the noise in the room, it also allows students to ask for help without halting progress in the way that raising their hand might.

EQUITABLE PRACTICES

No one wants to admit that their teaching style is biased toward one group or another, but to some degree, it probably is. Pay attention to who you are calling on, or better yet, try to use a randomizer whenever possible. Small, unintentional inclinations can quickly add up to be a big deal for some groups of students.

Plan lessons with everyone in mind. Try not to exclusively use sports metaphors, and don't try to pander to girls with lessons about hair dryers and makeup. Remember that some students prefer competition, while others prefer a cooperative challenge. An equitable classroom is achieved through variety. Listen to your students, ask them what they're interested in, and adjust accordingly.

15

The Elementary Pathway

Keep in mind that even big-budget movies for this age group tend to be much shorter than those made for preteens and beyond. Very young students do well with short bursts of material that is repeated often, rather than epic exposure to new experiences.

KINDERGARTEN AND FIRST GRADE

At this age level, students are struggling with empathy and putting themselves in the place of other characters. This limits the ability to use "control a character" style coding environments. Also, many (including Kiki) don't believe that it's appropriate to have students this young on a computer every day. For this reason, K–1 is prime time for language and concept building, logic practice, game playing, and sequence generating. Use unplugged curriculum like Real Life Algorithms* or Fuzz Family Frenzy* to inspire this age group.

Kindergarten and first-grade student takeaway: *Computer science is a thing, and it's fun.*

SECOND AND THIRD GRADES

Students in this group are ready to have some authentic **block-based** coding experiences. We still recommend that seven- to nine-year-olds have limited computer time, keeping exposure to about thirty minutes per session, one or two sessions per week.

With the developmental progress these students have made, they should now be ready to predict what their character will do when a few lines of code are run. Students this age can also understand when simple sequences are messed up and organize them into the right order.

> **Block-based programming**: Drag and drop layout, where code fits together like puzzle pieces, making skilled typing and strict attention to syntax unnecessary.

Some of the challenges with this age group can be their lack of persistence, failure to read directions, and distractibility. Use a blend of focused coding games like Lightbot* and The Foos*, as well as unplugged activities like My Robotic Friends* to help fine-tune their skills.

Second- and third-grade student takeaway: *Computer science is something that I can do and enjoy.*

FOURTH AND FIFTH GRADES

Here is where the computer starts working its way into CS education as a fundamental tool. A lot will change with your elementary schoolers between the beginning of fourth grade and the end of fifth grade. This is also the age where you really want to inspire your students, both to help them see the beauty and power of CS and to fortify them against the STEM slump (Modi, Schoenberg, & Salmond, 2012) that can happen in middle school.

The first thing that needs to happen here is a build-up of self-efficacy. In the fourth grade, students should be encouraged to explore projects that interest them and they should not be expected to jump straight into "memorize and repeat" types of assignments. Step-by-step tutorials with frequent brain breaks (like CS Fundamentals*) work well for this.

Next, students should be gradually ushered into a creative environment where they can begin to program stories and games and explore options for customization. Scratch* is fantastic for this stage.

Finally, toward the end of the fifth grade, most students who have engaged in block-based programming will be ready to gently shift into text-based programming. Tools like Pencil Code* (pencilcode.net) allow students to do just this.

Make sure you set aside time to teach internet safety and digital citizenship to students of this age. Other elements of computer science can be introduced to this group, too. Consider exposing fourth and fifth graders to interface design and user testing!

Fourth- and fifth-grade student takeaway: *Computer science is something that I can use to create stuff.*

OUT-OF-SCHOOL LEARNING IN THE ELEMENTARY GRADES

With all of our discussion of the K–12 pathway, we must take care not to miss a very promising and potent opportunity . . . out-of-school time!

Out-of-school time offers great opportunities for informal learning. Providers of after-school programs, summer camps, and clubs are generally allowed to set their own pace and cover topics that interest students, without burdening children with assignments or tests. This makes the after-school setting a great place to foster a *love* for computer science, instead of just an understanding of it.

If your school has yet to adopt computer science into the regular program, then after-school instruction may be your best bet. Not only will you provide access otherwise denied to your students, but their excitement could be the critical factor in convincing others that CS deserves time in the school day.

Program providers treat out-of-school time opportunities differently depending on the age of children they serve. Some elementary after-school programs double as child care, and providers strive to keep students engaged without turning the time into extended schooling. Other programs are dedicated to a single topic and invest quite a few hours over a short number of days. Both have to deal with the uncertainty of how frequently any given child will show up over the course of a module.

In grade school, aftercare classes can include students from a wide variety of grades and levels of maturity. A span of six years would be a lot for any age group, but it's a great divide when that span represents more than half a child's age. There is much to manage with a grade school CS program, but it is one of the most magical experiences an instructor and students can have. With their great imaginations and access to computers to use as "mud pies"—stuff to think with—young kids will create more inventive games, animated stories, and apps than adults could ever dream up.

Let's start with the good news. Grade school students generally don't have a very deep understanding of what computer science is. This makes it far less intimidating for a new CS instructor to teach. Everyone can learn together! This is a perfect opportunity, too, to call on high school and college CS students to volunteer. Not only will they share their love of technology, but they will gain experience explaining concepts at a very basic level, which really anchors their understanding of computer science.

Young students also tend to be more adventurous and less afraid of failure than their older counterparts. This means we can generally ask them to try new things without them worrying about what other students in the group are doing. Grade school students will eagerly follow your prompt to create a rudimentary program where one character says "Hello, world!" and another says "Hi" back. Not only will they do it, they will celebrate their success and might even have the thrill of accomplishment that carries them through subsequent bouts of frustration.

One of the downsides to working with elementary after-school clubs is the frequency of tears. Young kids can be tenderhearted. Maybe they don't understand one of the words you used. Maybe their neighbor got a turn first. Maybe they're getting hungry and really wish their mom was around to hold their hand. Whatever the reason, young students can have a meltdown at the strangest times, especially when confronted with failure, which is a regular element of learning CS. A teacher needs to toggle between compassion and tough love when working with this age group, especially when the class is not mandatory and students can opt in or out from week to week.

Another difficulty with this group is the wide range of developmental capabilities on display. Some students won't even be able to read, whereas others will see a user interface and instantly understand what needs to be done. It's impractical to think that you can keep students moving in lockstep in a grade school club. Providing "edutainment" may need to be the central mission, meaning students spend the majority of their time being simultaneously educated and entertained.

As you plan an after-school program for students in K–5, keep the following advice in mind:

1. Choose lessons that require minimal preparation for teacher or student

Starting with lessons that require hours of preparation is a sure-fire way to become overwhelmed and feel you are unprepared for the journey ahead. Look for lessons that are self-guided or are simple to prepare and execute. Examples that fit these criteria are presented in the elementary pathway section starting on page 111, but here's a quick summary:

We suggest starting out with some unplugged lessons, moving on to online games that teach skills, trying out a few concept-strengthening tutorials, then finishing with an open playground that lets students test out what they have learned.

You can find an "unplugged" lesson for almost any CS concept out there. Prepping for an unplugged lesson might require only gathering some playing cards or printing photocopies, and watching a streaming video about what to expect with the activity. For online coding lessons, seek applications that walk students through a task step-by-step, providing all the context, instruction, and vocabulary they need, just at the right time. If you insist on more in-depth lessons, partner with a more seasoned instructor who can model the activities or otherwise provide helpful advice. (Once you've taught an activity several times, you'll be motivated to enlist more teachers and in the process help grow the ranks of capable instructors!)

Students will not want to put in a lot of time preparing before they get started, either. Because nothing is worse than coming to an exciting learning experience only to be asked to wait for others or listen passively for long stretches, let kids get busy with "bell ringer" or "warm-up" activities right away. The excitement of digging right in is great, and sometimes it's hard to tear kids away from the fun. Let students know in advance how long their "warm up" period will be so they will be mentally ready to transition into the day's learning.

2. Don't count on students attending each and every lesson

Because participation in out-of-school programs can be so irregular, it's hard to count on having each student attend each and every session. For this reason, seek stand-alone lessons that don't require prior experience. If a single lesson or project spans six sessions, students who miss every other session will quickly find themselves in a place where they simply can't keep up.

3. Students may not be able to work on projects at home

Some instructors assume they can introduce an activity in class and let students finish at home if time runs out. This is not practical for many families. Even if students have a computer and internet access at home, they may not be allowed screen time during the week, or their home obligations might keep them wrapped up for too long to mess with activities that parents see as optional.

If you enjoy giving assignments that allow students to extend themselves beyond what is possible in the scope of a single session, consider making a second session available each week just for playing with ideas that students have already learned. If this isn't possible, then schedule a couple of "loose end" days into the program calendar.

4. Students get bored doing the same things week after week

Students like to feel like they're making progress, so if the activities they're working on feel too similar week after week, they will start to mentally check out. Keep your club fresh by changing up the coding environment every three or four lessons.

5. Students' interest and attention span for education at a computer maxes out around thirty minutes

This can be difficult to remember, especially with how immersed some students will become and how loudly some will complain when it's time to shut things down. Truthfully, young students shouldn't be expected to spend more than thirty minutes at the computer at a time anyhow, and even that period should be broken up by at least one body-moving brain break.

If you have longer than an hour each day to learn, consider breaking the session into twenty- or thirty-minute chunks where you start out with an unplugged activity, move into an online option, then wrap up either by sharing or involving students in writing or art projects that solidify what they learned that day. This will keep computer time feeling special and accommodate all types of learners.

6. Pair programming is a *must*

Not every learning activity needs to be done in tandem, but lessons that take place at the computer are best learned with at least two kids at each screen. When working with partners, students are more likely to think through challenges as they arise, rather than halting all progress until the teacher comes to the rescue.

Remind students that talking about a problem out loud can sometimes trigger a solution in their mind.

7. How many times each week will the class work on computer science?

This question is important, because it sets the stage for what you can accomplish over a set period of time. If you're going to be working only once each week, you will effectively have less than five hours of computer time over the course of a ten-week club. Even if students came in with all of their foundational knowledge and were able to use that five hours without interruption, they still wouldn't have enough time to create a magnum opus from start to finish. In this situation, keep expectations in check by working on short, self-contained projects each week instead.

If your plan is to visit CS three or more times a week, then you will likely find that you have more time to luxuriate in creativity. Spreading a project or two over multiple sessions is more plausible when only a small amount of computer time is available every day.

8. Can all students read?

If the answer is yes, you will have a much easier time finding lessons that appeal to everyone, but if the answer is no, there is still hope! There are several activities appropriate for prereaders and these can make for a fairly robust early learner curriculum. Just covering Code.org's CS Fundamentals through Course 1 could take prereaders through an entire school year's worth of lessons. For more variety, add lessons that rely on active feedback and animations to get concepts across. The Foos by codeSpark is a great one, as is Lightbot. (Learn more about each of these in the following pages.)

9. Are we just doing this for fun, or do we want a product at the end?

The last question that you need to consider is *why* you are taking on CS. If you just want to raise students' confidence for computer science (which, by the way, is an *excellent* reason to do this), then spend more time on lessons, tutorials, and games. If, on the other hand, you want students to come out the other side having built a portfolio project that showcases their knowledge, you'll need to pack the fundamentals in at the beginning so there is plenty of time for creation at the end.

Whatever your final approach, remember that the number one most crucial thing to address at this age is enjoyment. If students are going to hate computer science forever because of one bad experience, it's better they not be exposed to it at all.

Elementary Computer Science Resources

Here are more resources to explore, followed by an elementary lesson plan called "Build an Alligator!"

CS Fundamentals by Code.org *(Ages 5–15)*	
"Students will create computer programs that will help them learn to collaborate with others, develop problem-solving skills, and persist through difficult tasks. By the end of this course, students create their very own custom games or stories that they can share."	https://studio.code.org
https://code.org/educate/curriculum/elementary-school#overview	

The Foos by codeSpark *(Ages 4–8)*	
"codeSpark has created a unique and powerful approach to teaching computer science built on cutting edge research and hundreds of hours of prototype testing. codeSpark's learning games are designed with no words so even prereaders and ELL [English language learning] students can play and learn from our powerful curriculum. "By playing our games, your students will improve their critical thinking skills, and improve in other disciplines, all while having a lot of fun!"	http://goo.gl/EtBALt
http://www.thefoos.com/wp-content/uploads/2015/11/Full_Curriculum.pdf	

Bitsbox by Bitsbox *(Ages 6–8)*

"With Bitsbox, children learn to program by creating fun apps that work on computers and gadgets like iPads and Android tablets. The Bitsbox.com website provides each child with a virtual tablet and a place to type their code. The experience starts with lots of guidance, first showing learners exactly what to type, then quickly encouraging them to modify and expand their apps by typing in new commands."

https://bitsbox.com/teachers

https://goo.gl/ 7hKbPg

Tynker by Tynker *(Ages 6–14)*

"Tynker's online courses provide a complete learning system with interactive exercises, guided tutorials, fun creativity tools, puzzles and more to make programming fun."

https://www.tynker.com/school/courses/index

https://goo.gl/ It8KvU

Scratch Creative Computing by ScratchEd *(Ages 8–14)*

"Get Started! Begin your creative computing experience by downloading the guide.

"The guide can be used in a variety of settings (classrooms, clubs, museums, libraries, and more) with a variety of learners (K-12, college, and beyond). No prior experience with computer programming is required, only a sense of adventure!"

http://scratched.gse.harvard.edu/guide/download.html

http://goo.gl/ nCU8m9

Lightbot by Lightbot *(Ages 6 and older)*

"Students play the initial set of 'Basic' levels in Lightbot. They will learn how to tell a computer what to do with a series of basic commands and gain the general process by which computer programs are written."

https://lightbot.com/Lightbot_BasicProgramming.pdf

https://goo.gl/ E2GkIl

This lesson plan is available for download at resources.corwin.com/ComputationalThinking.

Modified with permission from codeSpark. Written by Joe France.

Program: The Foos	Video	Worksheet
Cross-Curricular Ties: Design Thinking	bit.ly/FooGator	bit.ly/FooGator Worksheet
Age Range: 5–9		
Duration: 45–60 minutes		
Scan the QR Code or copy the link to see additional curriculum elements.		

FIGURE 15.1 Screengrab, Coding With the Foos: Build an Alligator Challenge!

Source: Modified with permission from Code Spark. Written by Joe France.

Overview

This lesson challenges students to apply their programming knowledge to build a simple timing game. Students will sequence different commands together in a loop and learn how small changes in code can result in big changes in the computer's behavior and how fun the game is. Students may then adapt this pattern in new contexts.

Vocabulary

Sequence: The step-by-step order of a set of instructions

Loop: A command that repeats a set of instructions over and over again

Parameters: Settings that change the behavior of commands

Lesson Objectives

Students will be able to:

- Sequence commands for a specific behavior
- Use a loop to repeat behaviors
- Explain outcomes of code variations
- Explore and explain design choices

Materials and Resources

- Tablets with *The Foos*
- Whiteboard or projector

Prerequisites

Players must have access to the loop, hide, and wait commands.

Preparation

1. Read the lesson.
2. Watch the video at http://bit.ly/FooGator in preparation to show it to your class.
3. Create a new level in Foo Studio and follow along with the instructions in the video.
4. Download or print out the Worksheet at http://bit.ly/FooGatorWorksheet to use with your whiteboard or projector.

Activity

Step 1. Introduction

Begin with a group discussion of what players have learned about sequences, loops, and parameters.

Show them the icons for the **hide** and **wait** commands. Ask them what they think these commands do.

TABLE 15.1 Some of the Computing Concepts Introduced in "Coding Withe the Foos"

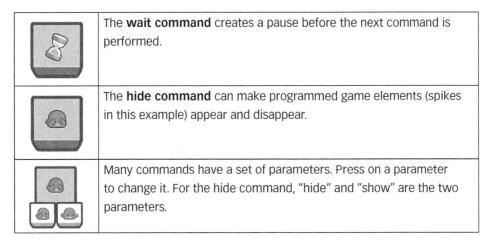

	The **wait command** creates a pause before the next command is performed.
	The **hide command** can make programmed game elements (spikes in this example) appear and disappear.
	Many commands have a set of parameters. Press on a parameter to change it. For the hide command, "hide" and "show" are the two parameters.

Step 2. Building—Show your class the video at http://bit.ly/FooGator, and then have them follow the instructions for creating the alligator.

- Students will need to pause the video when placing the blocks of their alligator—the video is sped up.
- Encourage students to play their level when the video does. Remind them that coding is a process consisting of the following steps:
  - The coder thinks of something she wants to do.
  - The coder tries to figure out how to get the computer to do it.
  - The coder writes code that he thinks will work.
  - The coder tests the code to see if it works.
  - If the code doesn't work, the coder investigates to find out why.
- Have students publish their level when they are finished.

Step 3. Discuss together—Get the class's attention and ask:

- What was the most challenging part of the activity?
- Why does the video use two wait commands?

Put the worksheet on the projector. Discuss:

- What would each of the following sequences do? ***Answers:***
  - *Sequence 1—The spikes would appear and disappear quickly.*
  - *Sequence 2—The spikes would disappear and never come back.*

- o *Sequence 3—The spikes would disappear quickly.*
- o *Sequence 4—The spikes would disappear and reappear three times and then stop.*
- o *Sequence 5—The spikes would appear for longer.*

- **Design Thinking**—Which of these would be fun for the player? Could any of these sequences lead to an unfair game for the player? *(Different answers are okay. Get students to explain why they think one way or another.)*

Step 4. Remixing—Have your students make a new level, and have them attempt one of the following challenges:

- **Different Animal** *(for students who struggled with the exercise)*—Get them to repeat it again, but make a different toothy animal.
- **Coding Challenge**—Code a second type of spike so it alternates appearing and disappearing with the first one.
- **Design Thinking Challenge**—Use the same code sequence, but apply it to blocks, hearts, gems, and enemies. Have your students think about whether it makes the game more fun or more frustrating.

Step 5. Real World Wrap Up—Show, hide, and wait are used in many places in computer science. Whenever a video is paused, a coder had to program the video player so it will wait until the play button is pressed. Even when typing, most cursors blink on and off—show, wait, hide, wait, and repeat—just like the spikes.

- **Challenge** students to look for times when a wait command is being used in an app or a game.

16

The Middle School Pathway

In middle school, a variety of conditions affect when and how computer science (CS) fits into the master schedule. Lasting anywhere from a term to a year, middle school CS may be required or offered as an elective. Elective classes might meet anywhere from once a week to every day. Whatever the case, one *good* CS class is all an enthusiastic student needs to prepare for high school.

A great year-long middle school class would incorporate hardware, robotics, networking, internet safety, and at least one solid term of programming. A CS course for students of this age needs to strike a delicate balance. It needs to be thorough enough that students are confident and prepared for more intense study down the line, but it needs to be light-hearted and flexible enough that it doesn't intimidate.

For middle school students, their entire world is changing. Many of them are transitioning from the fun freedom of elementary school and are struggling to build the responsible habits they will need for high school. Beyond that, most hit puberty somewhere in their sixth- to eighth-grade year. These developing hormones can lead many to start focusing more on their social concerns than their intellectual development, which can hinder their desire to try new subjects—especially those that seem, on the face of it, to be complicated or hard. On the plus side, by middle school, students can distinguish opinion from fact and weigh options, which means that a good teacher stands a chance when it comes to encouraging preteens toward new experiences.

Projects are a great way to include both rigor and whimsy, while also encouraging inquiry-based learning. At the time of this book's publication, there are a few sets of middle school curricula* being developed with these ideas in mind. To get started right away, examine JavaScript Road Trip* (javascript-roadtrip.codeschool.com) and Codecademy* (codecademy.com), two self-guided coding tutorials that are appropriate at this age level.

OUT-OF-SCHOOL TIME IN THE MIDDLE GRADES

In-class time isn't the only way for students to get started with CS. Many informal, community-based CS learning opportunities are available for middle school students. Let's focus some attention on after-school clubs.

Spanning the needs and interests of middle school students is tricky. Some students will be looking forward to CS club because they're interested in the subject (and have been for a long time), whereas others are just becoming curious to learn what CS is about and might just want to make an app or learn to fiddle with web pages. Some students won't know what CS is at all when they show up for their first day, and they may think they're signed up to spend hours playing games or creating graphic design projects.

Depending on how many times a week you meet and how long you are together for each session, you can plan on students achieving varying levels of experience. A club that meets for two hours every weekday for a semester can power through much more than a club that meets once a week for an hour.

Although middle school students are generally ready for a broad survey of CS subjects in a year-long class, after-school clubs will likely be more successful if each term is advertised as a stand-alone opportunity. Going term by term gives you more recruiting opportunities, too. That kid who didn't participate in the first round can be recruited again some weeks later. Ten weeks of robotics will draw a different crowd than ten weeks of hardware or ten weeks of app building. For the remainder of this section, we will assume ten-week programs, at an hour and a half each week.

A smooth entry is imperative if you want to retain a diverse range of middle school students. You should try to engage the newcomers, while not boring or deterring the veterans. Simply explaining the different starting points of those involved can serve to fortify the class against the bumps and struggles of the first couple of meetings.

It can also be helpful to send out a survey on the first day to gauge the comfort level of everyone involved. This survey can also be used as a pre/post test to show traction in learning and interest should you want to work toward getting middle school CS courses adopted in local schools.

Pair programming is particularly useful for students in grades 6 through 8, as it encourages an environment of collaboration and helps to lift students who might otherwise feel self-conscious about their abilities. For those who aren't used to working in pairs, there might be some hesitancy to share both glory and responsibility, but don't give in to the pleas of the independent. Working together is as vital a skill in the tech industry as the ability to create meticulous code . . . possibly more so.

In the beginning, even middle schoolers can benefit from unplugged activities and block-based languages. These introductory activities connect new concepts to familiar real-life ideas and give students conceptual grounding they can connect back to when the struggle becomes real. They also provide a sense of whimsy to a subject that students unfamiliar with computing can find intimidating. Starting the first three meetings with unplugged activities before moving to an online tutorial with a similar concept lends strength to the exercise and helps ideas stick.

By the end of the first month, students will be able to move on to an environment that is suited for their comfort level. If your group feels ambitious but their skills are shaky, keep moving forward with a block-based interface, like MIT's App Inventor 2* (ai2.appinventor.mit.edu). If students are ready to transition into a text-based language, try Code.org's App Lab* (code.org/applab), which lets kids swing back and forth at their leisure. If, however, your students are chomping at the bit to begin writing code, you might want to consider a more thorough tutorial environment, like Treehouse* (teamtreehouse.com). Treehouse has a fee associated with full membership, but at the time of this printing, their trial period is two free months, which is plenty of time for students to move past the "beginner" phase.

Round out your club by making sure each student makes an app they can share with their friends. All of the environments listed above allow students to create sharable artifacts. Note that while the App Inventor creations are suitable only for an Android device, almost all web-based JavaScript apps will run on any smartphone that can launch a browser.

Middle school student's takeaway: *Computer science is useful to me, and I can be one of the people creating tools and resources that others use.*

Middle School Computer Science Resources

Check out these comprehensive resources for middle grade students, and then give the lesson "Input and Output" a try.

Bootstrap	http://goo.gl/ Rc2G5t
"Bootstrap integrates math and computing education to enable equitable access to and success in both subjects for all students in grades 6–12. We design our curricula, pedagogy, and software in tandem to foster learning at depth and to ease adoption. Our high-quality professional development programs and classroom materials reflect our core belief in the value of human teachers."	
http://www.bootstrapworld.org	

Project GUTS	http://goo.gl/ v1gE9f
"Project GUTS—Growing Up Thinking Scientifically—is a science, technology, engineering and math (STEM) program for middle school students based in Santa Fe, New Mexico and serving districts nationally. Growing up thinking scientifically means learning to look at the world and ask questions, develop answers to the questions through scientific inquiry, and design solutions to their problems."	
http://www.projectguts.org	

Project Lead the Way	https://goo.gl/ V0Xbce
"Through topics like coding and robotics, flight and space, and DNA and crime scene analysis, middle school students engage their natural curiosity and imagination in creative problem solving. PLTW Gateway is a strong foundation for further STEM learning in high school and beyond, challenging students to solve real-world challenges, such as cleaning oil spills and designing sustainable housing solutions."	
https://www.pltw.org/our-programs/pltw-gateway/gateway-curriculum	

Computer Science Toolkit and Gaming Course by Microsoft Research	http://goo.gl/ SgHdu0
"The Computer Science Middle School Toolkit (CS Middle School Toolkit) contains three tracks of lessons: science and games, mobile apps and social impact, and puzzles and programming."	
http://research.microsoft.com/en-us/collaboration/focus/womenincomputing/tools-to-learn-cs.aspx	

CS Discoveries by Code.org	https://goo.gl/ E2s0g9
"CS Discoveries is designed from the ground up to be an accessible and engaging course for all students, regardless of background or prior experience. By providing students opportunities to engage with culturally and personally relevant topics in a wide variety of CS related fields we hope to show all students that CS can be for them."	
https://code.org/educate/csd	

This lesson plan is available for download at resources.corwin.com/ComputationalThinking.

Original Lesson

Program: App Lab by Code.org	
Age Range: 13–15	https://goo.gl/ 2GJZcK
Duration: About an hour	
Scan the QR Code or type the URL to go to App Lab.	

Overview

The fortune teller is a classic activity, bringing many amazing elements of CS together into one simple and impactful program. In this exercise, students will use arrays (ordered lists) to store possible answers for "yes or no" questions.

Lesson Objectives

- Get students programming in a simple interface
- Practice debugging to keep their program in working order
- Follow steps to bring their design to life on a computer

Materials and Resources

- Pens or pencils
- Paper
- One to two dice
- Computer with internet

Vocabulary

Array—A list of elements bundled together under one name and organized one after another

Element—A single item in a group

Index—The number given to show the positioning of an element in an array or list

List—In this context, another word for an array

Preparation

As a group, pull students in front of the chalkboard or document camera and tell them that you are going to create your own personal fortune tellers. First, since everyone likes to hear their news in different ways, we will work together to gather a list of possible answers.

Ask for ways to answer a "yes or no" question. You can start the list out for them:

["Yes!," "No."]

(Note: The square brackets, quotes, and commas are vital if you plan to take this to the computer lab following the unplugged portion.)

As students offer additional (appropriate) answers, add them to your list until you have six. If you are using two dice, you can add twelve. Your list might look something like this:

["Yes!," "No.," "Maybe.," "Perhaps!," "Ask again later.," "It is unclear."]

Now, add a number (index) below each possible answer, so that students can choose one at random, based on what the die returns. On the computer, indexing starts at 0, so 0 = "Yes!" and 5 = "It is unclear." How will your students ever get "Yes!" returned when rolling a die that goes from 1 to 6? Pose the question to them and see what they come up with!

Now, ask for volunteers to offer "yes or no" questions. You may have to request that they keep them appropriate and respectful. Pass the die around the room and have students roll to show the answer. Example:

- "Will I be rich?"
- Roll die = 3
- (3 – 1 = 2)
- The element with the index of 2 is "Maybe."
- Have the whole class shout out the answer.

Do this several times until everyone understands how to use a random number to find an element by index in an array.

Finally, have the students grab a piece of paper and write their own (respectful) array for their own fortune teller.

Activity

Get your class to the computers and open up AppLab (studio.code.org/projects/applab). Students can make their own accounts if they would like to return to their projects another day. Accounts are not required, however.

The first thing your students will need to do is make sure that their workspace is on "design" mode (Figure 16.1).

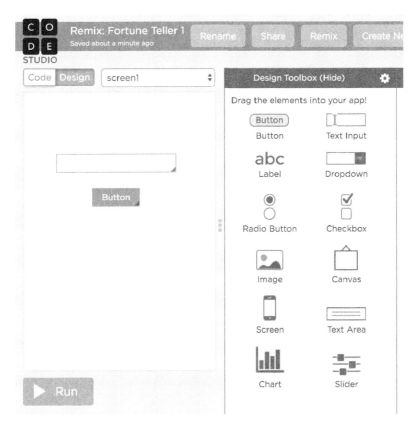

FIGURE 16.1   Design Mode in AppLab

Students will need to:

- Drag a "Text Input" area out to the screen and note the name given
- Drag a "Button" out to the screen and note the name given
- Customize the attributes of each item on the screen as desired

Next, it's time to program. With the button highlighted, click on the "Events" tab, then underneath "Click" click on "Insert and show code" (Figure 16.2).

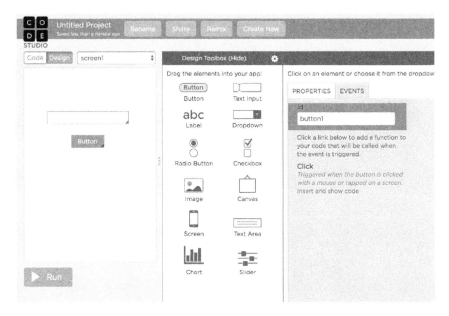

FIGURE 16.2 Edit Properties and Events for Design Elements

Now we see the existing code as blocks (Figure 16.3)!

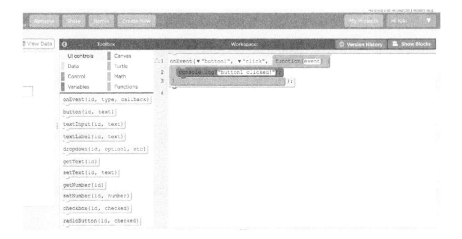

FIGURE 16.3 Using Blocks to Program the Fortune Teller

You can easily switch between blocks and text using the "</> Show Text" button (Figure 16.4).

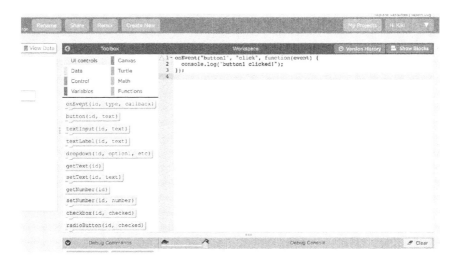

FIGURE 16.4 Program in Text View

You can drag blocks from the Toolbox in either mode, and the code will render itself into the whatever format you're currently looking at.

Now, we need to add the code to make our button populate the textbox with an answer. It's worth letting the class browse around to figure out how to do this specifically, but ultimately, they will need to:

- Create a list variable where they enter all of the answers they wrote down earlier
- Set the text of the textbox to an item of that list, noted by **nameOfList[n]** where n is a random number produced by the **randomNumber** function in AppLab

  (The above all needs to be done inside the "event" function already provided.)
- Let students tailor and customize their boxes and buttons (or even add images) if they have extra time.

Figure 16.5 shows an example of the finished code. Pretty slick, eh?

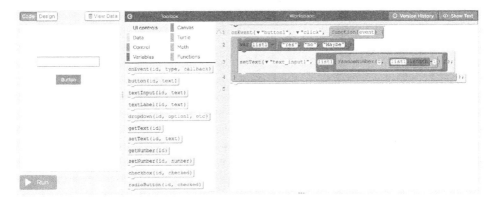

FIGURE 16.5 Completed Fortune Teller Program in AppLab

Wrap Up

Let students go around and look at one another's projects.

- Did anyone do something totally out of the ordinary?
- How did your students feel about AppLab?

What It's All About

AppLab is a bridge between block-based coding languages and the text-based language JavaScript. At the time of this writing, JavaScript is the most used programming language around. Head over to githut.info to see where it ranks now!

If your students already know how to create web pages, they can copy the code that they wrote here and paste it directly into their website, where they can guide their own buttons and text boxes!

To see a running version of this app, visit: https://goo.gl/bkTJhA

17

The High School Pathway

In theory, one year of high school computer science should be enough for a typical student to learn how to put a rough program together, especially if the student has already traversed the pathway laid out previously. This doesn't mean that the average student will retain all of the ins and outs of computer science, but that's okay.

By ninth grade, students should understand how the puzzle pieces of CS fit together to build programs. This first year of high school can open up a whole new world of innovation and relevance as far as programming is concerned. By dreaming up their own creations, then investigating how to build them, students will learn a lot about how computing works in the real world.

Self-guided learning is necessary but not sufficient at the high school level. By this point, students may have developed into coders, but they won't be able to cross over that thin line to becoming programmers until their skills have been polished and they can tell a **tree** from a **stack**. There are techniques and nuanced practices computer scientists must learn and be able to draw on if they want to take their work to the next level. That's why teacher involvement is crucial for this age group.

Tree: A top-down data structure with a linear organization where information is both added and removed from the same end.

In the past decade, Exploring Computer Science (ECS) has become the go-to curriculum for high schools wishing to offer introductory CS. Designed with a sharp eye on equity and grounded in inquiry-based learning, ECS is a tested and validated course suited to classrooms serving students from diverse backgrounds. It presumes no prior experience, which is different from traditional courses, which blast straight into programming and often leave behind the average uninitiated kid.

Stack: A data structure with a linear organization where information is both added and removed from the same end.

ECS provides an engaging first look into computer science for high school–age students. ECS is a yearlong course designed to be personally interesting and socially relevant to students in any community. Topics covered in ECS include **human–computer interaction**, problem solving, web design, programming, computing and data analysis, and robotics. Along the way, students also come to understand how computers and the internet work.

For those with their eye on Advanced Placement options, the College Board has designed the Computer Science Principles (CSP) course with the goal of "creating leaders in computer science fields and attracting and engaging those who are traditionally underrepresented."

Although CSP is often referred to as a single, cohesive course, it is really more of a *framework* on which courses can be structured. Code.org, Project Lead the Way, The Beauty and Joy of Computing, Mobile CSP, Thriving in our Digital World, and many other groups have created curricula that aim to satisfy this ideal. Like the ECS course, many lessons contributed to the course are highly interactive. (What a nice thing in an AP course!) One example? An interactive "unplugged" activity about the internet has students transferring objects from person to person, emulating how electronic data, or *packets*, are routed through a network.

Other programs, like Google's Computer Science for High School* (cs4hs.com) and Advanced Placement Computer Science A* (http://goo.gl/iaQtMr), make great choices when looking into a full-year option for grades 9 through 12.

These programs are thorough and amazing, but what if a teacher wants to bring a few days or weeks of CS to their classroom without having to add something new to the course catalog? Good news, there are a huge number of options there, too!

Nearly all of the programs listed for middle school are equally powerful at the high school level. Even Scratch, which is a youthful, block-based language, will get the imagination flowing in high school teens. Beyond these, dozens of one-off, subject-tailored activities can be found in curated CS pages, like the "teacher-led" activity page on Code.org (code.org/educate/curriculum/teacher-led).

OUT-OF-SCHOOL TIME IN HIGH SCHOOL

Again, different students will turn out for computer science club depending on the targeted subject and how you advertise. If you are trying to engage a diverse group of students, be very clear about your starting requirements and end goals. For example, a poster that states "Coding Club: Make apps you can share with friends for free. No experience needed!" will appeal to a broader group than one that says "Computer Science Club: Learn how to use JavaScript on an Android emulator without any compiling!"

Some of the advice so far may seem intuitive, but here's some that is not. While teaching at the University of Oregon, Kiki found that underrepresented students tended to gravitate toward the more relaxed instructors . . . or rather, they tended to shy away from the instructors who felt the need to constantly demonstrate their own intelligence and expertise. After taking notes on students' favorites (and years of checking RateMyProfessors .com), it became clear that instead of seeking out the most accomplished or confident mentors, students newer to computer science tend to seek out instructors that are more approachable.

This story should serve as a cautionary tale for teaching young adults: don't overteach. You may have graduated summa cum laude and be able to describe every nuanced difference between a function, method, and procedure, but is this going to help a young Latina discover her love for coding? If the answer is no (it is probably no!), then try listening more, speaking less, and allow your students to make their own mistakes. After all, getting into and back out of trouble is half the fun of programming.

Now it's time to put some thought into an after-school curriculum for high school students. At this point, let's assume you are working with a semester-long coding club that meets two days a week, for an hour and a half. Unfortunately, this rules out a thorough journey into the amazing Exploring Computer Science, Computer Science Principles, and even CodeHS* programs, since they were developed for use every day for a full year. A savvy teacher could always pull favorite lessons from any of these curricula and modify them for a shorter time span (which is a fantastic idea!) but what about a teacher who is just beginning to explore the CS landscape?

Unplugged lessons are just as effective with young adults as they are with children, but the approach needs to be slightly different. When high school students show up to code, they can be put off or feel patronized if you toss them into the kiddie pool. On the opposite side, they can feel overwhelmed or unprepared if you toss them into a standard **IDE** (integrated development environment) and expect them to start programming right away. A good solution for this is to start their first experience with a "bring your own device" multimedia scavenger hunt. (A full 70 percent of teens own smartphones, so when they pair up, everyone should be covered.) After they've explored some of the programming landmarks, spend the next class actually building

IDE: Integrated development environment, where all of the useful components for coding live together in one software package.

something small (possibly adding to the framework of a program that already exists). Then, pull out unplugged lessons to illustrate the tricky concepts that emerged along the way. The activities from CS Unplugged* (http://csunplugged.org/), available for almost any CS topic, are great for this age group.

Dynamic web page: "Dynamic" web pages access information from a database, so to alter the content the webmaster may only need to update a database record.

By the end, make sure students have had time to develop at least one master project on their own or with a partner. Having an artifact they personally created to pass along and share with family, friends, and the world will help students believe they are capable of using CS to reach an end goal.

Some examples of completed projects could be:

- An Android app
- A **dynamic web page**
- A Python game*
- Consider hosting a showcase during your last week where students share their masterpieces to the community. Turn it into a fundraiser while you're at it! Set up in a local pizza parlor, and draw in the neighborhood to see what students can accomplish in a few short weeks after school.

High school student takeaway: *I understand the basics of computer science, can create a program from the beginning, and know how to locate resources to help me make something bigger and more impressive in the future.*

High School Computer Science Resources

These comprehensive curricula are all you need for high school instruction. Use of many of these programs is supported with professional development. Check them out and then give the "Homework Excuse Generator" lesson a try.

Exploring Computer Science	
"Exploring Computer Science is a yearlong course consisting of 6 units, approximately 6 weeks each. The course was developed around a framework of both computer science content and computational practice. Assignments and instruction are contextualized to be socially relevant and meaningful for diverse students."	 http://goo.gl/ XFnbcy
http://www.exploringcs.org/curriculum	

CodeHS	
"CodeHS is a comprehensive program for helping schools teach computer science. We provide web-based curriculum, teacher tools and resources, and professional development."	**https://goo.gl/ ht9AM4**
https://codehs.com	

Computer Science Principles	
"The course introduces students to the foundational concepts of computer science and challenges them to explore how computing and technology can impact the world. The AP Program designed AP Computer Science Principles with the goal of creating leaders in computer science fields and attracting and engaging those who are traditionally underrepresented with essential computing tools and multidisciplinary opportunities."	**https://goo.gl/ 8yYtPH**
https://advancesinap.collegeboard.org/stem/computer-science-principles/curricula-pedagogical-support	

App Inventor 2 by MIT	
MIT offers a full set of curriculum for their block-based programming environment. With separate courses for game development, app development, and companion curriculum for CSP, App Inventor 2 is an accessible way to get a head start in computer science.	**http://goo.gl/ G960kV**
http://appinventor.mit.edu/explore/resource-type/curriculum.html	

Computer Programming by Khan Academy	
"Our Intro to JS courses teaches the basics of programming in the JavaScript language, using the ProcessingJS library on top for drawing and animation. That means that we teach all the basic concepts in the language, but our use case for them is visual. For example, when we talk about nested for loops, we demonstrate how we can make a grid of gems on our screen."	**https://goo.gl/ HEFmvT**
https://www.khanacademy.org/coach-res/reference-for-coaches/teaching-computing/a/programming-curriculum-overview	

This lesson plan is available for download at resources.corwin.com/ComputationalThinking.

Original Rendition of a Classic

Language: JavaScript	
Cross-Curricular Ties: Math	https://goo.gl/11bR4s
Age Range: 12–18	
Duration: 30–60 minutes	
Scan the QR Code to see an example of what your students will make.	

Overview

Dice games are classics when it comes to having fun with your family, but they are also classics when it comes to introducing computer science! Programming dice can be a great way to get a huge impact with minimal coding. This is one of the reasons that dice lessons make their way into almost all entry-level coding classes. Here, we provide a small twist on one of our favorites.

Lesson Objectives

- Learn to read basic JavaScript
- Use random numbers to simulate dice
- Identify mathematical techniques in existing code
- Use the Web to teach themselves additional JavaScript commands

Materials and Resources

- Paper
- Pens or pencils
- Dice (up to 3)
- Computer with internet

Preparation

Play a quick guessing game with your students.

- Ask students to predict what number you are going to roll on a die.
- Roll the die.
- Ask whether it was the number that they predicted.
- How did you know it wouldn't be a 0? How about a 10?
  - Six-sided dice have a known minimum and maximum number.
- How could I roll a 10?
  - Roll more than one die.

Tell students that they will be building their own dice game on the computer. Using a few lines of JavaScript, students will simulate having their computer roll dice, then alert them as to what they rolled. Here's the catch: Students will be teaching themselves!

Guide students to the "Roll the Dice" project page located at https://goo.gl/btu63T. This will give them all that they need to investigate their way through their first steps at coding. It will even guide them to JSFiddle.net, which is an all-in-one online coding platform that will let them write JavaScript immediately.

Activity

Turn students loose with their first JSFiddle program, located at https://jsfiddle .net/ya8srgar. This, combined with their guiding Google Doc will give them all they need to play around for the day. Their programs have some great comments and examples to help illustrate what they're supposed to be doing.

Once they move on to the second program, at https://jsfiddle.net/xqxznb2m, they will have blanks where they need to copy what already exists into a new context. This is great for helping them branch out and try some coding on their own.

Finally, they'll fork off their own program and choose three challenges from the provided Google Doc. Giving them the freedom of choice will allow them more ownership over their education, as will turning them loose to find the answers using a search engine. There's no shame in finding examples of others solving problems that you're working on in the early stages of coding . . . or the late stages, for that matter!

For your convenience, samples of the JavaScript exercise have been provided at the end of this lesson.

Wrap Up

JavaScript is a fantastic language for writing applications for any platform. Whether on a Mac, PC, or a smartphone, practically anyone can pull up a JavaScript site.

This exercise was meant to illustrate the exploratory nature of programming. Often, you'll need a little kickstart, but if you're brave enough to venture out on your own and try new things, you can discover quite a lot without formal teaching. This is *vital* to the world of computer science.

Have a discussion around this idea with your class. Here are some other questions to prompt their thinking:

- How did you feel when you first saw the code?
- Did it help to go through everything line by line?
- Were you tempted to look up other coding concepts to make your program do something new?
- What were you most afraid of?
- Were you able to get over that fear?

What It's All About

Computer science is all about learning to learn. Don't be afraid to make your class struggle. Just be sure to be open and honest about the frustration that comes with learning something new, and help them understand that at some point, this is hard for everyone!

Code From Doc

https://jsfiddle.net/ya8srgar

```
// This is a comment. The computer doesn't run it, but humans can read it.
// Use comments to describe what you are about to do
// Let's use a *variable* to set the minimum number on our die to 1
var myMin = 1;
// Now we need to set the max to 6 for a 6-sided die
var myMax = 6;
// Time to program the first die using random numbers
// (random is already in the Javascript library)
var die1 = Math.floor(Math.random() * myMax + myMin);
// Now we add the command to shout out the number we rolled.
alert("You rolled the number "+ die1);
```

- How do you think you run the program given in the window?
- How would you fork off your own version to play with?
- Try going through the code line by line to see if you can figure out what everything does.
- Can you change the min and max to make your own custom die?
- How might you save or update your program to keep your changes?

https://jsfiddle.net/xqxznb2m

```
// This is a comment. The computer doesn't run it, but humans can read it.
// Use comments to describe what you are about to do
// Let's use a *variable* to set the minimum number on our die to 1
var myMin = 1;
// Set a new max so we can roll a 12-sided die
var myMax = 6;
// Time to program the first die using random numbers
// (random is already in the Javascript library)
var die1 = Math.floor(Math.random()* myMax + myMin);
// Let's add a second die using the same min & max
var die2 = ;
// Can you add a third die with the same parameters (min & max)?
// Now add all of the dice to the alert.
alert("You rolled the number "+ die1 + " and a " + die2);
```

- Don't forget to fork off a copy.
- Can you finish adding die2 to the program?
- Can you add all of the code for the variable die3?
- How can you get them to show up in the alert?

https://jsfiddle.net/wugzov8y (Sample of what students might create)

```
// This is a comment. The computer doesn't run it, but humans can read it.
// Use comments to describe what you are about to do
// Let's use a *variable* to set the minimum number on our die to 1
var myMin = 1;
// Set a new max so we can roll a 12-sided die
var myMax = 12;
// Time to program the first die using random numbers
// (random is already in the Javascript library)
var die1 = Math.floor(Math.random()* myMax + myMin);
// Let's add a second die using the same min & max
var die2 = Math.floor(Math.random()* myMax + myMin);
// And a third die using the same min & max
var die3 = Math.floor(Math.random()* myMax + myMin);
// Add a sum to keep track of the total score for the turn
var dieSum = die1 + die2 + die3;
// Now add all of the dice to the alert.
alert("You rolled "+ die1 + ", " + die2 + ", and " + die3 + ". Your
total score is " + dieSum);
// added an if-statement here
if(dieSum > 25){
alert("You got lucky!");
}
```

- Can you figure out how to have each die use its own min & max?
- How would you create a new variable to hold a sum of the three dice?
- Can you search the internet for "javascript if-statement" to figure out how to check to see if the sum of the dice is larger than 25 and then pop up an alert if it is?
- Can you figure out how to tell if any die is less than 6, and if so, reroll?
- How would you figure out if the sum of your dice is even, and if it is, pop up an alert?
- Can you add a fourth die that always rolls the same thing as one of the other dice?

18

Adapting Lessons for Your Class

Throughout this text we have presented fun and fundamental lessons to help you and your students get started with computational thinking, programming, and computer science (CS). It's likely you've found plenty of lessons on your own as well. Some will be perfect for your needs as they are, but it's likely many are less than turnkey solutions. Try not to let a few snags ruin what could otherwise be a useful lesson. People have different interests, and different genres suit different situations. Just like in the movie industry, rewrites are often in order! Find a plot that speaks to you and tailor it to suit your needs.

Here are a few ideas for adapting lessons to fit your class:

1. THE LESSONS ARE ONLY SUGGESTIONS

You know your classroom best. If a lesson seems to be written in a very specific, detailed manner, it's most likely because the author wants it to be easy to read and implement, not because it can't be taught any other way.

For example, let's say you're working with an unplugged lesson that asks you to pick a random number from a deck of cards, but your classroom can't use cards because the students like to throw them like ninja stars. See if you can adapt the lesson to use dice instead. Can't use dice because the district worries that it promotes gambling? Cut strips of paper and label them with the numbers you need.

Similarly, if you find that a Scratch lesson is calling for a pig that throws fireballs and your school has a zero tolerance policy on weapons, substitute a bird that drops sticks or a fish that spits bubbles. Small details like this rarely have any effect on the concept behind the lesson.

2. ADAPT A LESSON FOR YOUNGER STUDENTS

Many CS lessons are designed for older students. This doesn't mean that prereaders are altogether incapable of learning the material, only that they need a little extra assistance. If you're planning to use an unplugged lesson with younger students, you may want to take two class sessions to complete it instead of only one. Make sure you spend a good amount of time going over examples as an entire class before splitting students into groups, so that they know what they're supposed to be doing.

Prereaders are also often able to use online environments that claim to be beyond their aptitude. Just make sure you plan a class session to teach students how to use the mouse and keyboard, and count on assignments taking two or three times as long at first, as students figure out what code blocks do (since most won't be able to read the provided labels).

When teaching very young children, let go of the idea that you need to cover every element of a lesson. Instead, find one main takeaway and make that the focal point of your activity. Use physical activity and stories from life to drive home an idea whenever possible.

3. ADAPT A LESSON FOR OLDER STUDENTS

There are some excellent lessons for entry-level CS students, and many of them sound like they were created for children who are quite young. Don't let this deter you from sharing an activity with an older class. What may take young kids an entire class period might turn into a great warm-up activity for older students. You might also find that you can bundle two or more lessons together to get a more rounded experience.

If you find an online lesson that feels too infantile for your students, try to port it over to a more appropriate environment. Instead of using a unicorn in Scratch, try using a narwhal in App Inventor.

Adapting lessons can also be a great activity for students. Take some lessons meant for prereaders and offer them to your students for tweaking. Challenge them to bring the lessons up to par for their classmates, keeping the same concept but pumping up the intensity for students their own age. You might be surprised how helpful this can be in showing what groups understand, and where they are still weak.

When those lessons are done, take some of your favorites and share them on CS social media sites!

4. CREATE A LESSON TO SQUEEZE INTO OTHER CURRICULA

Not all CS lessons need to be large and complicated. Often, if you get in the habit of looking for opportunities, you can find small elements of class lessons that you already use that can benefit from a trip to the computer lab.

Whether you teach art, science, math, or music, CS affects the industry that your students are training for. Shouldn't it affect their education as well? Even if all you do is introduce a bit of coding a couple of times each term, students will begin to identify themselves as belonging to the greater world of CS.

As a math teacher, start with typical test questions. Take a word problem or equation and have young students program a story around it in Scratch or Tynker. Older students can write a utility to help with difficult mathematical functions using JavaScript or AppLab. Once the students are familiar with the overall environment, a bulleted list of challenges and their accompanying score should be enough to inspire brilliant work.

When teaching science, data can be your friend! Help students visualize interesting information using an online tool like Google Charts (https:// goo.gl/AqOGvI) or Vis.js (http://visjs.org). Try modeling the heat map of boiling water or ant colonies using NetLogo (http://www.netlogoweb.org). The usefulness of CS in science class cannot be overstated. Some of these tools seem complex, but a few hours of playing around with prebuilt examples will have you on the right track!

Art is a natural partner to CS. Whether you're generating images automatically with code using JavaScript, or illustrating a digital story in Alice (http://www.alice.org), there are dozens of ways to blend coding into art class. What project do you plan to work on next week? Try pairing one of your hands-on creations with some website work. Art and CS are an addictive combination, once you get started.

If you teach music, you practically already teach CS! Sheet music is a highly informative algorithm and switching between instruments is very similar to switching between programming languages. Digital composition programs like EarSketch (http://earsketch.gatech.edu) add a thrilling twist to both programming *and* music education, and Scratch has built-in beats and notes to inspire even the youngest of learners.

Whatever you teach, it's true that there can be a significant time investment when it comes to preparing your first coding-based lesson. Try to think of this as an investment, rather than a burden. After all, once you've created a lesson, you can use it again and again. Take a playful approach and mess around a bit on your own. Eventually, it will all click!

If you find yourself inspired, but perplexed, head on back to Chapter 4 and go through the warm-ups and exercises again. You just might notice that everything is a little clearer now than it was the first time around.

19

What People Are Doing and How They Are Doing It Well

The steady drumbeat for computer science (CS) in K–12 has grown louder over the past few years. It's possible that this new public attention being paid to CS is what caught *your* attention and motivated you to give computing a go.

Recognition of CS as a fundamental literacy is growing at the collegiate level, too, and not just in departments of computer science. Colleges and universities are incorporating computer science into biology, engineering, economics, finance, and astronomy, to name only a few majors. In fact, any subject concerned with big data, statistical analysis, systems, or modeling relies on CS to accomplish work and expand the discipline.

Take the Human Genome Project, which was completed by research universities in 2003 and still stands as the world's largest collaborative biology project. Without the computational power made possible through CS, determining the sequence of chemical base pairs that make up human DNA and mapping all of the genes would not have been possible. Further, the ability to predict, analyze, and cure diseases such as Huntingtons disease, cystic fibrosis, and some forms of breast cancer has benefitted greatly from the mash-up of biology, medicine, and computer science.

Increasingly, universities are preparing students to apply computational practices in the sciences, so familiarizing students in the years prior will make this a smooth progression.

One college that's leading the way is Harvey Mudd, a private college in Claremont, California, which focuses on mathematics, the physical and biological sciences, and engineering. At Harvey Mudd College every student, regardless of major, takes an introductory CS course. The course is not like most introductory courses, though. Instead of being a typical "one size fits all" offering, each major gets a CS class that has been tailored to that area of study. At Harvey Mudd an engineering major takes the

FIGURE 19.1   Fun Fact: There are approximately 20,500 genes in human beings, the same range as in mice. We wouldn't know this without computer science.

engineering-flavored CS class, a biology student takes CS designed for biology majors and a math major learns CS within a math context. Students apply computational methods to their investigations in their major, and not surprisingly, many end up with a dual major in computer science. In fact, with every student getting exposure to CS, enrollment patterns at Harvey Mudd are changing. Historically, 10 percent of Mudders in the CS major were women, and after five years of this CS-for-all approach, the department graduates a steady 40 percent female CS majors. By comparison, the national average is stalled at 18 percent (Hill & Corbett, 2015).

Higher education institutions around the country, including Harvard University, the University of Washington, and the forty campuses of City University of New York, are following Harvey Mudd's lead, treating computer science as a general requirement for many majors. What should you take away from this? By exposing your students to computer science, you prepare them not just for CS but for college majors for which CS is integral. Help students to see interdisciplinary connections, and illustrate how subjects they are interested in studying relate to computing with recent innovations such as these ("How Computer Science Advances Other Disciplines," 2015):

- Veterinarians develop diagnostic apps for examining horses, literally in the field.

- Earth scientists worldwide collaborate to produce a global digital geological map, allowing virtual views of rocks underground, everywhere.

- Forensic specialists design on-person technology that turns the average FBI agent into a walking laboratory for hyper-fast crime scene analysis.

- Neurologists use feedback from the accelerometer in the Apple Watch to detect warning signs of seizure in people with epilepsy.

- Environmental scientists equip robotic fish with sensors to monitor water quality.

- Economists analyze popularity data from Amazon.com to predict public response to new products.

- Psychologists develop software that allows a paralyzed person to control a wheelchair by thinking a simple command.

- Researchers use three-dimensional computer analysis to help musicians improve their performance by comparing their posture and movements with the ideal.

- An English professor collaborates with a computer scientist to extract metaphors from scanned literature, resulting in a searchable database that allows people to study how metaphors have been used throughout history.

- Political scientists help improve the security of elections by applying computational science to examine thousands of ways a voting system can be attacked and then analyzing the effectiveness of countermeasures against those attacks.

As a thought exercise, ask students to imagine what might be accomplished through the mash-up between CS and things they care about. Here are a few challenges to prime the pump:

- Keeping park playgrounds clean and in good repair
- Connecting neighbors or making a neighborhood more walkable
- Reducing food waste
- Fighting wildland fires
- Predicting the spread of disease
- Helping older adults stay in their homes
- Making travel in bad weather safer

Take Note! The Verizon Foundation holds an annual competition called the Verizon Innovative App Challenge.* Students in Grades 6 through 12 can win state, regional, and national awards. Student teams accepting the challenge frame a problem they care about in such a way that a computer can help solve it. Once winning entries are selected, Verizon and MIT step in and build the apps students envisioned, making their solutions a reality. This is a great bridge from *think* to *thing;* students apply design and computational thinking skills to imagine great solutions, and aren't hampered by their lack of technical skills. Learn more at http://appchallenge.tsaweb.org.

TAKING IT TO THE STREETS: BUILD COMMUNITY ENTHUSIASM FOR COMPUTER SCIENCE

One way to build sustained support for computer science is by building your school's brand as a place where kids learn to code and think well. Go public and engage the community! Invite parents, grandparents, residents, and businesspeople in the neighborhood to school and show them first-hand what all the noise is about. The community will be as excited as you are and will want to contribute to your winning endeavor. Host a family coding event or hold a tech fair. Here are a few examples to emulate:

Host a family coding day. Gideon Hausner Jewish Day School in San Francisco hosts a K–8 Family Coding Day each December. During the inaugural event in 2013 (Patterson, 2014), more than two hundred people dropped in on a Sunday to explore computing with Gideon Hausner students. Racks of iPads, two computer labs, and several "unplugged" classrooms saw plenty of action with twelve distinct sessions. Each year the planning team, led by tech integration specialist Sam Patterson, prepares an array of age-appropriate workshops, some requiring computers and others not. Families register for workshops in advance using the event management platform, Evenium, and receive tickets and a map showing where sessions are held around the school. The team enlists parents and local technical professionals to help run sessions, but more and more often this charge falls to students.

Patterson says parents and grandparents leave Family Coding Day with a new appreciation for computer science. "What I cannot express is how much this event shifted the conversation about coding on our campus. Parents were able to experience what programming in an educational context is all about." They see students learn more than programming, too. Patterson notes, "They are surprised how empowered and confident students are."

Here are a few tips to take away from events like Gideon Hausner's Family Coding Day:

- If your school participates in the CSEd Week "Hour of Code," schedule the family event as a culminating celebration.
- As computer science becomes established in the general program, showcase activities that reflect the day-to-day curriculum. Show how computing supports the development of math, science, and communication skills.
- Involve kids at each step. They can contribute to planning and take leading roles during the event. When practical, have students run sessions.
- Extend resources by assigning one computing device to each two people. Encourage pair programming and "out loud" thinking.
- Further extend resources (and demonstrate that computational thinking doesn't require devices) by offering unplugged activities. Kinesthetic learning activities are sprinkled throughout this book.
- Schedule short sessions, forty minutes at most. Having brief sessions keeps the tone light and allows guests more opportunities to sample an array of computing activities.
- Minimize confusion and improve traffic flow by distributing tickets that include the activities folks registered for, rotation times, and a map marked with locations for each activity.

Hold a tech fair. The Tech Academy at Foshay Learning Center, a K–12 school in Los Angeles Unified School District, holds a tech fair each year. Seniors present projects they've worked on for an entire semester, projects that focus on solving real-world problems that they and people in their community care about. Sample projects include a Scratch-based water conservation game; e-textile and Arduino activities designed to build younger students' interest in science, technology, engineering, and mathematics (STEM); and projects dealing with domestic violence, sexual health, and even the "gamification" of school. The latter involved the development of a smartphone app students use to track and award badges for positive behaviors of others, such as an overheard kind word or spontaneous litter clean-up.

A lot happens on the way to the tech fair. Before getting down to work, students workshop ideas with each other and get critical feedback during "pitch" sessions with industry experts and community stakeholders. Once projects are ready, students rehearse their presentations during a practice fair.

Leslie Aaronson, lead instructor and recent Los Angeles Unified School District (LAUSD) teacher of the year, notes that students are more committed to producing quality work when they have to lay it on the line during the tech fair. "They work to a higher standard when they know someone else will examine their work," notes Aaronson (personal communication, November 30, 2015). Aaronson also sees the community becoming more invested in the school when they see what kids are doing. She says, "Parents see the complex projects their kids take on and get a sense there might be a future in tech ahead of them. I like to think it helps parents come to expect the best out of them."

Perennially, the tech fair serves as fertile meeting ground for companies interested in developing local talent. After the 2015 tech fair, Managed Career Solutions (a career development and job placement firm) teamed with Sabio (a tech training company) to offer free web development courses for recent graduates of Foshay Tech. Sabio cofounder Gregorio Rojas said, "We are proud of the students at the Foshay Tech Academy, and all the great work the school is doing to cultivate awesome diverse tech talent. We want to support and encourage these young tech innovators to aim for the fences" ("Sabio Gives Back," 2015).

The fair attracts interest from companies wishing to offer summer internships, too. By working with community partners, Foshay Tech Academy is able to provide real-world experiences and networking opportunities through which students develop technical skills and build otherwise hard-to-secure social capital. The winning team in 2015, Side With Peace, got a head start on their project during summer internships at PeerSpring, a civics and tech platform that helps students understand, apply, and master core skills through acts of citizenship. The Side With Peace team received laptops from Sabio, too.

Education leaders are responding to the Foshay experience as well. The Los Angeles school board president and high academic officials attended the tech fair and recognized Foshay for its innovative approach. Seeing Foshay Tech students in action, Jane Margolis, a key contributor to the highly regarded Exploring Computer Science curriculum, became motivated to design more professional development for teachers so they can use technology education to build social capital and encourage projects that contribute to the greater good of communities.

> **"***The term* social capital *emphasizes . . . a wide variety of . . . benefits that flow from the trust, reciprocity, information, and cooperation associated with human social networks. Social capital creates value for the people who are connected and—at least sometimes—for bystanders as well.***"**
>
> —Robert D. Putnam and Thomas Sander (2012)

TESTIMONIALS

You won't have to teach computer science for very long before you start seeing some major achievements from students. Often, this comes with considerable appreciation from parents, civic leaders, and the community. This section provides a handful of testimonials by educators who introduced their students to CS.

Tanya Cheeves, Forsyth School District, Cumming, GA

My personal story is one of meeting a first-grade Hispanic student who was just learning English. He was repeating first grade and was pulled out every day for several of the "support" programs (English as a Second or Other Language [ESOL], Individualized Education Program [IEP], Speech) our school district offers. He suffered from low self-esteem and was detached from his peers. In fact, his classmates had come to the conclusion that he understood and spoke little English because he was so withdrawn. I went into his classroom once a week this year to introduce computer science. He automatically took a keen interest in programming. It was as if a light bulb went on. His teacher stated that he felt successful in a school setting for possibly the first time. He came to school on Monday nights (ESOL Parent Night) and went straight to the computer to work on code—showing his parents and teaching his younger siblings what he could do. Computer science gave him purpose and hope. His teacher began to notice the problem-solving skills he was capable of applying to a variety of situations. Computer science offered him an outlet to show that language did not have to be a barrier or obstacle to his learning. Now, when he sees me in the hallway, he gives me a giant smile and a thumbs-up and says "CODE!" We share a common bond.

Alana Aaron, Wonder Workshop, http://blog.makewonder.com

This fall, Julainee developed a new passion. She was introduced to coding by her fifth-grade teacher, Alana Aaron. After she completed Code.org's CS Fundamentals Course 2, she did as many coding tutorials as she could and made friends with the robot duo, Dash and Dot from Wonder Workshop. "She spends her evenings hand-writing programs for Dash and Dot and brings them to school each morning, begging to put them into action," said Ms. Aaron (see Figure 19.2).

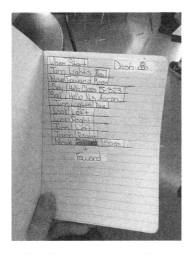 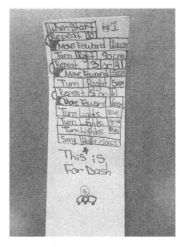

FIGURE 19.2   Blockly code Julainee wrote for Dash and Dot while at home.

Source: Lin (2015).

"What's most amazing about Julainee is that she has used her love of programming Dash and Dot to connect with and include students in our class who otherwise might not easily connect with other students. For instance, she wrote a script for Dash and Dot to star in our school Hour of Code kickoff video, and then worked with two autistic students to program Dash and Dot with their voices. She also included a student who recently arrived from Yemen and speaks very little English in the production of the video," Ms. Aaron said.

Elizabeth McCoy, President, Communities Rising

I thought you might be interested to hear how [Kiki's] Thinkersmith's unplugged activity, "My Robotic Friends," helped a team from rural south India, comprised of the sons and daughters of workers, win first prize in the Presentation Division of the First Lego League (FLL) Robotics regional competition in Coimbatore, India.

Each year, the FLL competition has a theme that teams must research and then make a presentation to the judges. This year's theme was education and required students to teach any topic they chose in a new and better way.

Our team chose the topic of computer coding and used the cups game presented in "My Robotic Friends" to teach the basics of computer coding and to show that coding can be taught to young children, without the use of computers and using a game format.

The judges were overwhelmed with our students' understanding of the basic concepts of coding and algorithms and the use of simple instructions to build various shapes made of cups to demonstrate the relevant concepts.

Our team members spent hours teaching other teams and their coaches, along with teachers and students from the host facility, The Indian Public School, the concept of "coding unplugged" and the idea that games can be used as valid educational tools—a relatively unknown concept in Indian education.

It was a truly remarkable ending to two days of competition, when our team, all from families living in severe poverty and the only government-aided school defeated twenty other teams from various private and international schools to win first prize in the Presentation category.

Communities Rising is a U.S.-based 501(c)(3) [organization] that provides quality educational opportunities for the rural villages in the Villupuram District, the poorest district in the Indian state of Tamil Nadu. Our students primarily come from families whose parents are day laborers. The average family of five survives on about $400 a year.

We teach English, math, computer education, art, and music to over 1,600 students in our afterschool and in-school programs. We are the largest provider of computer education for primary and high school students in our area. We have been teaching Lego We Do robotics for primary students at our summer camp for the past four years. We have participated in the FLL competition for the last two years and hope to make Lego robotics part of our regular secondary school curriculum when funding becomes available.

Following this experience, we intend to incorporate the Hour of Code into our computer education program. Although the villages where we work have no internet access, we plan to use as many unplugged activities as possible and download whatever materials we can.

Grant Hosford, codeSpark

The study of computer science has many benefits and some of my favorites are the least obvious. One such example is the empathy kids must have in order to create a program or game that others enjoy. At first students will be happy just designing things for themselves, but they quickly transition to wanting friends, parents, and others to enjoy their creations. Putting yourself in the shoes of the user is a powerful tool for product design and for life in general.

Professor Ben Schafer, University of Northern Iowa

I work with kids in the local Coder Dojo. We use the Hour of Code materials to introduce kids to the idea of programming and they then work through a variety of activities using Scratch. One of the very first activities that they do is to draw out their initials ala Logo.

One weekend I walked up to one of our newer students—an eight-year-old—who was just finishing up this assignment. I noticed that he had created a block called "half circle" and was using it in several places in his code. In the six months I had been working with the dojo I had never seen even our most advanced students look at how to "build your own blocks" in Scratch. So I asked him where he learned how to make this block.

He responded, "I have been going through the Code.org materials. In there we learned that a function is for code that you will use over and over again. I knew that I would make four half circles in drawing my initials and that's a lot of work. So I just went looking for how I could make my own function in Scratch."

I have to admit that my jaw dropped open in surprise. This eight-year-old not only gave me a nearly textbook definition of a function, but he understood the concept well enough to know when one should be used and could figure out how to make it happen.

Stories of transformative learning experiences in your classroom are just waiting to be told. If you need any more encouragement to get your students involved in CS, we suggest you just give them a taste. Their enthusiasm and inventiveness will be more evidence than we could ever provide to show you that CS is worth teaching. No more waiting in the wings, now—step out on the CS stage with your students and show the world what you've got!

Afterword

Opportunities Abound

You have reached the end of this book, but really, your journey has just begun!

If we've done our job, you are now wearing new lenses through which to view a world of new possibilities for your students. You've conducted thought experiments, tried out computing exercises, and examined various aspects of reasoning that underpin the coding experience. You've learned from movers and shakers in the world of computer science education and seen what kids can do with code. You've examined comprehensive curricula as well as low-bar learning activities you can pull off in an instant. Maybe, just maybe, you see how computing can live within and even amplify the subjects you teach. Taken as a whole, we hope you have a new idea of who is right for computing (everyone!) and feel motivated and ready to provide all your students with opportunities to learn computer science.

You are not alone in your journey. Professional development providers across the United States are preparing tens of thousands of teachers to teach new, inclusive introductory and Advanced Placement courses. Your efforts are the "glide path" into course offerings that are inevitably coming to your district. When you expose your kids to computing, they'll gain the confidence to sign up for those classes or drop into the nearest CoderDojo or community makerspace.

> **❝***An investment in knowledge pays the best interest.***❞**
>
> —Benjamin Franklin, statesman and inventor

Governors, mayors, chief executive officers (CEOs), philanthropists, and creative media and technology professionals are committing their support to schools and community hubs where kids learn to code. Broadcast the news of your school's activity so their support can find its way to you.

Opportunities to connect with like-minded souls are growing by the minute. Code.org keeps an up-to-date directory of school-age computing opportunities available across the nation. Check out what's happening locally and join in; your professional learning network (PLN) is as close as this URL: code.org/learn/local. Edcamps—local, participant-driven professional learning experiences created by educators for educators—are dipping into coding, too. Edcamps are held in every state and in twenty-three countries, with well over 50,000 teachers taking part. The Edcamp Foundation can help you get started: www.edcamp.org/attend. Join a distributed PLN, too. Connect with K–8 teachers on Twitter using the hashtag #csk8. If you teach high school, connect through the Computer Science Teachers Association hashtags #csta and #computerscience.

We hope we've left you wanting more ideas for resources and curriculum you can use for your own investigations into computing and with kids. However, if we were to present an exhaustive treatment here, this book would be double its length and out of date before the printer's ink was dry on the page. Visit our companion website for links to an up-to-the-minute compendium of worthwhile computer science resources: resources.corwin .com/ComputationalThinking.

With our final words, we'd like to say: Computer science is not a fad. It's a skill set. It's a way of thinking. It's the backbone of innovation and gives us tools to change the world. The box office numbers for computer science are surging, and it is in large part because of educators like you. Thanks for being a part of this twenty-first-century feature. We look forward to seeing the projects produced by you and your students in the school years to come.

Computational Thinking and Coding for Every Student

Discussion Guide

Jane Krauss

Kiki Prottsman

A downloadable version of this discussion guide is available at: resources
.corwin.com/ComputationalThinking.

Computational Thinking and Coding for Every Student offers both a rationale and practical steps for introducing computer science in school. The authors recommend discussing your ideas and experiences with fellow readers to foster professional learning and personal reflection. This discussion guide is intended as a starting point for collegial conversations. Connect with other teachers who are starting their journey. Whenever you come across a question that really makes you think, share your response on social media and let everyone share in your epiphany!

Discuss on social media!

- FB: www.facebook.com/groups/CodingInClass
- Twitter: @CTandCoding
- G+: https://goo.gl/R9Q429
- See the companion site for more: resources.corwin.com/ComputationalThinking

PREFACE

Skipped the preface, did we? Many readers skip past the front matter of a book and dive right into the first chapter. This might be a good time to go back and read it. It's short, so you and your colleagues (who also skipped it) can read it together! In the preface, the authors summarize the state of computer science education (it's booming) and describe the arc of the text. Think of the preface as a brief summary of both the context for and the context of the book.

1. The preface presents the recent shift from little to lots of momentum for computer science in U.S. schools. Discuss: What was your impetus to give computer science (or at least this book) a try? What piqued your interest? In what ways were your impressions about computer science confirmed or changed?

_____

_____

_____

_____

_____

_____

2. As you get ready to dive into this book, what are your greatest hopes about introducing computer science? Your greatest concerns?

_____

_____

_____

_____

_____

_____

CHAPTER 1. AN INTRODUCTION TO COMPUTER SCIENCE

1. In Chapter 1 you explored the processes for solving a sudoku puzzle in a methodical way. Did you get a sense of how a solution could be derived by applying computational thinking?

_____

_____

_____

_____

_____

_____

2. Algorithms are all around us. Discuss another activity or task you accomplish by carefully executing a set of steps. What instructions might you lay out if you emulated the process in a computer app?

_____

_____

_____

_____

_____

_____

3. You likely have a better sense now of what computer science is and is not. Pretend you are speaking to a parent or your school administrator. How would you describe the difference between learning to use computers and learning computer science?

_____

_____

_____

_____

_____

_____

CHAPTER 2. WHY KIDS SHOULD HAVE THE OPPORTUNITY TO LEARN

1. In Chapter 2 the authors present computer science both as a fundamental literacy and as a way for students to practice resiliency in problem solving. What lessons in the core curricula do you teach that draw on students' reasoning and logic? What parallels do you draw between those and learning experiences in computer science?

_____

_____

_____

_____

_____

_____

_____

2. The authors relate Seymour Papert's association of computers to mud pies as both being mediums to think with. How does your role as teacher change when your students are learning in open-ended and exploratory ways?

_____

_____

_____

_____

_____

_____

3. Chapter 2 concludes by pulling back from the classroom experience to consider the larger societal case for why more youth should follow a computing education and career pathway. What of this rationale resonates with you? Do you see introducing CS as a supplement to your program, or as an obligation?

_____

_____

_____

_____

_____

_____

CHAPTER 3. TRY YOUR HAND AT CODING

1. Whew! Because you worked through the exercises in Chapter 3, you are now more experienced in computer science than most teachers! Your computational thinking got a workout, too. Each exercise ended with journal questions–prompts to help you examine the experience. Refer to your notes and discuss your experiences and impressions. Did you have similar experiences? Or did some activities present greater challenges or result in greater rewards for some of you than others?

_____

_____

_____

_____

_____

2. Pair programming was recommended as a metacognitive strategy for evaluating and improving reasoning. Did you try it with these exercises? If so, in what ways did thinking aloud together affect the experience?

_____

_____

_____

_____

_____

_____

CHAPTER 4. GETTING STARTED IN THE CLASSROOM

1. As with any student experiences involving computers, educators need to pay attention to students' physical and social well-being when teaching computer science. Discuss the advice in Chapter 4, and describe what resonated with you the most. What explicit actions will you take now that you might not have considered before?

_____

_____

_____

_____

_____

_____

2. Another practical concern raised in Chapter 4 was accessing appropriate technology for a fulsome computing experience for your students. Think about your teaching and learning environment in terms of technology access. In what ways does it fall short, and what workarounds might you try? If adjustments involve others, how will you state your case?

_____

_____

_____

_____

_____

3. Authors offered suggestions for getting started with computing. Consider your technology access and personal readiness and discuss the curriculum choices you plan to make.

_____

_____

_____

_____

_____

_____

CHAPTER 5. DOS AND DON'TS OF TEACHING COMPUTER SCIENCE

1. Discuss which "dos and don'ts" advice was most useful to each of you. What other "dos and don'ts" came to mind?

_____

_____

_____

_____

_____

_____

_____

2. In what ways do any of these "dos and don'ts" apply to other subjects you teach?

_____

_____

_____

_____

_____

_____

_____

3. Do any of these "dos and don'ts" conflict with practices you should or shouldn't do in other classes?

_____

_____

_____

_____

_____

_____

CHAPTER 6. ACTIVITIES THAT FOSTER COMPUTATIONAL THINKING

1. Computational thinking is an approach to problem solving that backs up a few steps to encompass problem *finding* and problem *posing* as well. Have you thought about problem solving as a stage in a bigger process before now? With your fellow readers, think of a problem-solving activity in your regular curriculum that could be more robust if you didn't hand students a problem to solve but instead set up the conditions by which they become aware of and begin framing a problem to solve.

_____

_____

_____

_____

_____

_____

_____

2. There is great interplay between the elements of computational thinking one applies to the task of programming a computer. That said, teasing CT apart helps get at important features of the process. In Chapter 6, the authors recommend that you get comfortable calling out CT practices by name. Are these "pillars" making sense to you? Would you refer to them within computer science learning? Where are they evident in other subjects you teach?

_____

_____

_____

_____

_____

_____

3. Look at the everyday examples of each "pillar" of computational thinking in the table at the end of Chapter 6. With your reading buddies, challenge yourselves to think of several more examples for each pillar. Can you come to agreement on one best example for each?

_____

_____

_____

_____

_____

_____

CHAPTER 7. DECOMPOSITION

1. The authors state, "Decomposition is breaking a problem down into smaller, more manageable parts." Which of the activities in Chapter 7 is most suited to your students and would best get across this universal approach to problem solving?

_____

_____

_____

_____

_____

_____

2. Imagine you are explaining decomposition as a problem-solving method to your students. How would you describe the process, and what examples might you give that would resonate with the interests and life experiences of the particular age group you teach?

_____

_____

_____

_____

_____

_____

CHAPTER 8. PATTERN RECOGNITION (WITH PATTERN MATCHING)

1. Reflect on the "pattern matching" activities and lesson in Chapter 8, and discuss in what ways "pattern matching" is about extrapolation and paying attention to salient cues. How might pattern matching be put to use in examining routines in long division, trends in history, structures in music composition, or "tells" in a game of poker?

_____

_____

_____

_____

_____

_____

2. How does pattern matching help pave the way for abstraction (described in the next chapter)?

_____

_____

_____

_____

_____

_____

CHAPTER 9. ABSTRACTION

1. Abstraction is used extremely often, even though we normally don't call it out as such in everyday life. Can you think of times when you use abstraction effortlessly?

_____

_____

_____

_____

_____

_____

2. Say you were going to explain the process of making cookies first to a forty-year-old, then to a four-year-old. How would your abstraction differ? With whom do you think you would use the most abstraction? Why?

_____

_____

_____

_____

_____

_____

3. Can you relate the idea of abstraction back to computer science? How might it help make your work easier if you were trying to create one function that added $x + 5$, one that added $x + 2$, and one that added $x + 7$ (where x is a number given as input by the user)?

_____

_____

_____

_____

_____

_____

CHAPTER 10. AUTOMATION

1. The authors mention in Chapter 10 that automation isn't always about running things on machines. How might automation make something easier, even if you still have to do it by hand?

_____

_____

_____

_____

_____

_____

2. Algorithms and automation often go together. Can you think of a reason that you might need one without the other?

_____

_____

_____

_____

_____

_____

3. Refer back to that abstracted algorithm for creating cookies presented earlier in the discussion guide. Now, imagine you were going to translate

it for a bakery system. How would the algorithm be different if you were sharing instructions with adults versus children? What might that algorithm look like if you were trying to prepare it for automation?

_____

_____

_____

_____

_____

_____

CHAPTER 11. ACTIVITIES THAT FOSTER SPATIAL REASONING

1. Your introduction to spatial reasoning started with a story from Seymour Papert's childhood. He said, ""Gears, serving as models, carried many otherwise abstract ideas into my head." Describe a time in your own learning where associating a new or abstract concept to something in the physical world helped you reach understanding.

_____

_____

_____

_____

_____

_____

2. The authors posit that spatial thinkers aren't born; rather, they are made through sufficient experience. What advice in this chapter about "spatializing" your teaching are you likely to try? Why does this kind of activity have merit over other ideas?

_____

_____

_____

_____

_____

_____

CHAPTER 12. MAKING WITH CODE

1. The authors offer examples of inventive student work. They also say, "Making isn't about *stuff*. It's not even about the *space*. More than anything, making is culture and design thinking." Discuss ways you could infuse the maker spirit into your school program.

_____

_____

_____

_____

_____

_____

2. Together with your reading partners, go to Twitter and search the hashtag #makerED. What are maker-educators talking about? In what ways do their interests (or concerns) resonate with you?

_____

_____

_____

_____

_____

_____

3. The authors discuss pros and cons of making in school as well as issues around equitable access. If the topic of making came up in a staff meeting at school, what defense for, or argument against, making would you make?

_____

_____

_____

_____

_____

_____

CHAPTER 13. DESIGNING A CURRICULUM CONTINUUM ACROSS K–12

1. In Chapter 13 the authors discriminate between computer science and digital literacy. Some teachers believe graphic design or word processing fall into the category of computer science. What elements of computer science can you imagine children could learn in classes like this (or even music and physical education) if teachers were to infuse CS vocabulary and concepts into these non-CS classes?

_____

_____

_____

_____

_____

_____

2. Clearly, if students can learn CS from "unplugged" lessons, then computer science involves more than programming. In what way do you think students who have learned CS have an advantage in their other studies over students who have not?

_____

_____

_____

_____

_____

_____

CHAPTER 14. IMPORTANT IDEAS ACROSS ALL GRADES

1. Some students fight the idea of working as part of a team. How would you explain the benefits of pair programming to reluctant students to help them understand it's an aid to learning, and not a punishment?

_____

_____

_____

_____

_____

2. Some teachers feel they aren't doing their job if they spend time standing back and observing, rather than actively teaching and helping. What are some of the pitfalls of jumping in to assist students too soon? What might be the benefits of holding back direct help and instead providing guiding questions and resources so students help themselves? What percentage of each style of helping do you do in your teaching? What percentage would you like this to be?

_____

_____

_____

_____

_____

_____

3. What ideas do you have to share to make stronger learners in a computer science environment? What can you do to promote equity in CS? If you have a study group, share some of your favorites with one another. Otherwise, head over to our Facebook page to have a meaningful discussion.

_____

_____

_____

_____

_____

_____

CHAPTER 15. THE ELEMENTARY PATHWAY

1. This chapter discusses unique challenges when teaching computer science to elementary school students. In your experience, are there any pertinent developmental milestones that the authors failed to consider? What would you suggest others take into account when trying to teach CS to young students?

_____

_____

_____

_____

_____

_____

2. Sometimes students in grades K–5 pick up concepts faster than adults do. (Think about how this is true with languages or complex remote controls.) How would you take advantage of their agile thinking in your classroom?

_____

_____

_____

_____

_____

_____

3. When you teach computer science and computational thinking to young students, it changes the way they look at problems in other subjects as well. What are some of the perks and pitfalls of having children learn to think like computer scientists?

_____

_____

_____

_____

_____

_____

_____

CHAPTER 16. THE MIDDLE SCHOOL PATHWAY

1. Middle school students are a rare breed. Not yet adults, but no longer wanting to be treated like children, this age band can be difficult to bring on board with new ideas. What are some of your best techniques for encouraging buy-in when introducing new topics to middle school students? How would you present the computer science value proposition?

_____

_____

_____

_____

_____

2. Middle school classrooms show a huge disparity in the computer science background of their students. How might you address wide differences in a way that strengthens everyone, rather than treating some students as remedial and others as advanced?

_____

_____

_____

_____

_____

_____

3. In what ways can you tailor your instruction to appeal to the "What's in it for me" nature of middle schoolers? Can you use this mechanism to encourage students to be positive with one another (both in class and online)?

_____

_____

_____

_____

_____

_____

CHAPTER 17. THE HIGH SCHOOL PATHWAY

1. High school students are starting to open their eyes to the world around them and investigate not only ways that they can get help from their community but also ways that they can be of help. Do you think your high schoolers would respond better to an activity that you have preplanned to benefit an actual end user in their neighborhood or to an activity that they are allowed to design themselves?

_____

_____

_____

_____

_____

2. Many students will be able to easily leap into text-based coding at this age, but some will struggle. Block-based coding is a simple way of building a foundation, but it has its limitations. How can you utilize different skill sets to keep all students moving in an upward direction without anyone feeling like they are hindered by the learning pace of others?

_____

_____

_____

_____

_____

3. When working in groups at this age, you will find that some students position themselves so they don't need to do any coding at all. In what ways might you structure your projects so that everyone gets to experience "taking the wheel," while keeping coding anxiety to a minimum?

_____

_____

_____

_____

_____

CHAPTER 18. ADAPTING LESSONS FOR YOUR CLASS

1. With a new subject such as computer science, you might be uncomfortable straying from teaching a lesson the way it is written. If you find that you need some tweaks to an otherwise great lesson plan, what do you plan to do? Share your resources with our online community on Facebook. Also, Tweet away!

_____

_____

_____

_____

_____

2. Sometimes lessons need more than a little alteration for a particular group of students. Choose one of the lessons from the book (or find one online) and with your reading partners, practice "fixing" it for your needs. Share your adapted lesson with our online community so they can benefit from your work, as well!

_____

_____

_____

_____

_____

_____

3. What might you do when you recognize that you have the perfect place to squeeze in a computer science project but cannot find a lesson that even comes close to hitting the mark for your particular grade or subject? Will you attempt to create one on your own? Will you ask for help from our community? Would you feel comfortable assigning your class the task of coming up with a project and then assigning them to complete that project?

_____

_____

_____

_____

_____

_____

CHAPTER 19. WHAT PEOPLE ARE DOING AND HOW THEY ARE DOING IT WELL

1. Chapter 19, with stories and testimonials from the field, was meant to inspire. Which story or testimonial spoke to you the most? What was it about the teacher, learner, or community experience that made it meaningful?

_____

_____

_____

_____

_____

_____

2. If you were to host an event to foster community support for your school's computer science program, what would you do? What would you be asking of the community? (Beyond monetary support, could this include volunteer time, tours of industry, or participation in career fairs?) How would you present the value proposition to make the most of a well-timed and well-advertised fundraiser?

_____

_____

_____

_____

_____

_____

3. Do you have any students with testimonials? Have you heard any from your local community or any online communities that you belong to? We would love to have you share those with us! Please post any outstanding student experiences (positive or otherwise) to our online group. Please share on social media to your worldwide neighborhood of educators and make computer science education better for everyone!

_____

_____

_____

_____

_____

_____

_____

Glossary

Abstraction: Ignoring certain details in order to come up with a solution that works for a more general problem.

Algorithm: A list of steps that can be followed to carry out a task.

Automation: Controlling a process by automatic means, reducing human intervention to a minimum.

Block-based programming: Drag and drop layout, where code fits together like puzzle pieces, making skilled typing and strict attention to syntax unnecessary.

Computational thinking: Using special thinking patterns and processes to pose and solve problems or prepare programs for computation. Notably, decomposition, pattern matching, abstraction, and automation.

Computer science: The study and use of computers and computational thinking to solve problems.

Conditional: Block of code that can only run under certain conditions.

Debugging: To track down and correct errors.

Decomposition: Breaking a problem down into smaller, more manageable parts.

Digital divide: Inequalities perpetuated by disparate access to computers and the internet.

Dynamic web page: Dynamic web pages access information from a database, so to alter the content the webmaster may only need to update a database record.

Event-driven: A program model that allows a user to interact with and change the flow of the program using mouse clicks, key presses, and other actions.

Function: A piece of code that you can call over and over again.

Genius hours: Dedicated class time for students to explore their own passions.

Growth mindset: The personal belief that one's intelligence is not innate and fixed but develops through effort.

Human–computer interaction: Observing the ways humans interact with computers and designing technologies that let humans interact with computers in new ways.

IDE: Integrated development environment, where all of the useful components for coding live together in one software package.

If statements: Sections of code that run only if a defined set of conditions is met.

Loop: A set of instructions to be repeated until a condition is met.

Maker movement: A trend in which people gather in a shared workspace equipped for the invention and fabrication of unique products.

Pair programming: An agile software development technique in which two programmers work together at one computer. The "driver" writes code while the "navigator" reviews and advises on code as it is typed. The two programmers switch roles frequently.

Parameter: An extra bit of information passed to an abstracted function that allows it to create something more specific.

Pattern matching: Finding similarities between items as a way of gaining extra information.

Programming environment: A software workspace made for creating code.

Pseudocode: Instructions that look like they could be a computer program, but they are easier to read and don't necessarily follow rules of any language.

Self-efficacy: A person's belief about his or her own abilities to learn, complete tasks, and reach goals.

Software patch: A piece of software designed to update or fix a computer program.

Spatial reasoning: The ability to generate, retain, retrieve, and transform well-structured visual images.

Stack: A data structure with a linear organization where information is both added and removed from the same end.

Tree: A top-down data structure that organizes information using a root at the top and subtrees that hang from the root.

Unconscious bias: Unconscious assumptions based on experiences, social norms, and stereotypes that affect our beliefs and actions.

Unplugged: Computer science learning activity not requiring a computer.

Variable: A placeholder for a value that can change.

WYSIWYG: Pronounced "wizzywig," literally, "what you see is what you get." Common in web development, this refers to editing in a mode that looks like the final result, but information is actually being translated into code.

References

2015 Essential facts about the computer and video game industry. (2015, April). Retrieved from the Entertainment Software Association website: http://www.theesa.com/wp-content/uploads/2015/04/ESA-Essential-Facts-2015.pdf

Ackermann, E., Gauntlett, D., Wolbers, T., & Weckström, C. (2009). *Defining systematic creativity in the digital realm.* Billund, Denmark: LEGO Learning Institute.

Adams, S. (2015, February 17). The highest paying in-demand jobs in America [Web log post]. Retrieved from http://www.forbes.com/sites/susanadams/2015/02/17/the-highest-paying-in-demand-jobs-in-america/#6e4ca4222856

Ashcraft, C., & Breitzman, A. (2012). *Who invents IT? An analysis of women's participation in information technology patenting.* Retrieved from www.ncwit.org/patentreport

Brooks, J. G., & Brooks, M. G. (1993). Classroom tips: Teaching with the constructivist learning theory. In *In search of understanding: The case for constructivist classrooms.* Alexandria, VA: Association for Supervision and Curriculum Development.

Burrows, L. (2013, January 27). Women remain outsiders in video game industry. *The Boston Globe.* Retrieved from https://www.bostonglobe.com/business/2013/01/27/women-remain-outsiders-video-game-industry/275JKqy3rFyl T7TxgPm03K/story.html

Children and parents: Media use and attitudes report. (2015, November 20). Retrieved from Ofcom website: http://stakeholders.ofcom.org.uk/market-data-research/other/research-publications/childrens/children-parents-nov-15/

Code.org. (2016). *Promote computer science.* Retrieved from https://code.org/promote

Computer Science Fundamentals for elementary school [Curriculum]. (2015, March). Retrieved from https://code.org/educate/curriculum/elementary-school

Cool coding apps and websites for kids. (n.d.). Retrieved from Common Sense Media website: https://www.commonsensemedia.org/lists/coding-apps-and-websites

Cyberbullying Research Center. (n.d.). Resources for educators. Retrieved from http://cyberbullying.org/resources-educators/

Ehrlich, S. B., Levine, S. C., & Goldin-Meadow, S. (2006). The importance of gesture in children's spatial reasoning. *Developmental Psychology, 42*(6), 1259–1268.

Foundations for success: The final report of the National Mathematics Advisory Panel. (2008). Washington, DC: U.S. Department of Education.

Friesen, S., & Scott, D. (2013). *Inquiry-based learning: A review of the research literature.* Retrieved from http://galileo.org/focus-on-inquiry-lit-review.pdf

Fromberg, D. P., & Bergen, D. (2006). *Play from birth to twelve: Contexts, perspectives, and meanings.* New York, NY: Routledge.

Gerstein, J. (2013, July 23). STEAM and maker education: Inclusive, engaging, self-differentiating [Web log post]. Retrieved from https://usergenerated education.wordpress.com/2013/07/23/steam-and-maker-education-inclusive-engaging-self-differentiating/

Harkinson, J. (2015, July 2). The combined black workforces of Google, Facebook, and Twitter could fit on a single jumbo jet. *Mother Jones.* Retrieved from http://www.motherjones.com/mojo/2015/07/black-workers-google-facebook-twitter-silicon-valley-diversity

Heines, J., Ruthmann, A., Greher, G., & Maloney, J. (2012, August 6). Making music with Scratch session handout. Retrieved from http://scratched.gse.harvard.edu/resources/making-music-scratch-session-handout

Herlocker, J. L., Dietterich, T. G., Forbes, J. B., & Maritz, P. (2012). *U.S. Patent No. 8126888 B2.* Washington, DC: U.S. Patent and Trademark Office.

Hill, C., & Corbett, C. (2015). *Solving the equation. The variables for women's success in engineering and computing.* Washington, DC: American Association of University Women.

Hlubinka, M., Dougherty, D., Thomas, P., Chang, S., Hoefer, S., Alexander, I., & McGuire, D. (2013). *Makerspace playbook* (School edition). Retrieved from Maker Media website: http://makered.org/wp-content/uploads/2014/09/Makerspace-Playbook-Feb-2013.pdf

How computer science advances other disciplines. (2015). Retrieved from http://www.mtholyoke.edu/~blerner/Applications.html

Images of computer science: Perceptions among students, parents and educators in the U.S. (Google & Gallup Report). (2015). Retrieved from http://services.google.com/fh/files/misc/images-of-computer-science-report.pdf

Intel International Science and Engineering Fair (Intel ISEF) awards. (n.d.). Retrieved from https://student.societyforscience.org/intel-isef-awards

Lenhart, A. (2015, April 8). *Mobile access shifts social media use and other online activities.* Retrieved from http://www.pewinternet.org/2015/04/09/mobile-access-shifts-social-media-use-and-other-online-activities/

Lieberman, J., & Chilcott, L. (Producers). (2013, February 13). *What most schools don't teach* [Video file]. Available from https://www.youtube.com/watch?v=nKIu9yen5nc

Lin, J. (2015). Wonder Workshop. Retrieve from https://blog.makewonder.com/what-happens-after-the-hour-of-code-cb727ef95ac0#.59dh5rp77

Machaber, E. (2014, December 10). President Obama is the first president to write code [White House Web log]. Retrieved from https://www.whitehouse.gov/blog/2014/12/10/president-obama-first-president-write-line-code

Maiers, A., & Sandvold, A. (2014). *The passion-driven classroom: A framework for teaching and learning.* New York, NY: Routledge.

Martinez, S. L., & Stager, G. (2013). *Invent to learn: Making, tinkering, and engineering in the classroom.* Torrance, CA: Constructing Modern Knowledge Press.

Modi, K., Schoenberg, J., Salmond, K. (2012). *Generation STEM: What girls say about science, technology, engineering, and math* (Girl Scouts Research Institute Report). Retrieved from http://www.girlscouts.org/content/dam/girlscouts-gsusa/forms-and-documents/about-girl-scouts/research/generation_stem_full_report.pdf

Monitor height and position guidelines. (2008). Retrieved from ErgoCanada website: http://ergocanada.com/ergo/monitors/monitor_height_guidelines.html

NCWIT by the numbers. (2016, March). Retrieved from the National Center for Women in Technology website: https://www.ncwit.org/resources/numbers

Newcombe, N. S. (2010). Picture this: Increasing math and science learning by improving spatial thinking. *American Educator, 34*(2), 29–35, 43.

Oddy, S. (2015, February 3). Verizon's Innovative App Challenge names "Best in Nation" winners. Retrieved from http://www.verizonwireless.com/news/article/2015/02/verizons-innovative-app-challenge-names-best-in-nation-winners.html

Papert, S. (1980). *Mindstorms: Children, computers, and powerful ideas.* New York, NY: Basic Books.

Patterson, S. (2014, November 14). Create a family coding day for hour of code [Web log post]. Retrieved from http://www.edutopia.org/blog/family-coding-day-hour-of-code-sam-patterson

Pretz, K. (2014, November 21). Computer science classes for kids becoming mandatory. Retrieved from http://theinstitute.ieee.org/career-and-education/preuniversity-education/computer-science-classes-for-kids-becoming-mandatory

Previous years—Google Science Fair. (n.d.). Retrieved from https://www.googlesciencefair.com/en/competition/previous-years

Programming = better math skills + fun. (2014, May 8). Retrieved from http://www.tynker.com/blog/articles/ideas-and-tips/programming-better-math-skills-fun/

Putnam, R. D., & Sander, T. (2012). About social capital. Saguaro Seminar: Civic Engagement in America, John F. Kennedy School of Government at Harvard University. Retrieved from https://www.hks.harvard.edu/saguaro/socialcapitalprimer.htm

Rabin, M. O. (2012, July 10). *Turing, Church, Gödel, computability, complexity and randomization: A personal view* [Video lecture]. Retrieved from http://videolectures.net/turing100_rabin_turing_church_goedel/

Sabio gives back during the holiday season at Foshay Tech Academy in LA [Web log post]. (2015, December 10). Retrieved from http://blog.sabio.la/2015/12/sabio-gives-back-during-holiday-season.html

Santana, A. D. (2013, July 18). Virtuous or vitriolic. *Journalism Practice, 8*(1), 18–33. Retrieved from http://www.tandfonline.com/doi/abs/10.1080/17512786.2013.813194?journalCode=rjop20

Searching for computer science: Access and barriers in U.S. K-12 education (Google & Gallup Report). (2015). Retrieved from https://services.google.com/fh/files/misc/searching-for-computer-science_report.pdf

Smith, M. (2016, January 30). Computer science for all [White House Web log post]. Retrieved from https://www.whitehouse.gov/blog/2016/01/30/computer-science-all

Steps in a design thinking process. (2009, August 1). Retrieved from https://dschool.stanford.edu/groups/k12/wiki/17cff/Steps_in_a_Design_Thinking_Process.html

Stigler, J. W., & Hiebert, J. (2009). *The teaching gap: Best ideas from the world's teachers for improving education in the classroom.* New York, NY: Free Press.

The top six unforgettable cyberbullying cases ever. (2013, April 23). Retrieved from http://nobullying.com/six-unforgettable-cyber-bullying-cases/

U.S. Bureau of Labor Statistics. (2015, December 17). 2014 Median pay. *Occupational outlook handbook: Computer and information technology occupations.* Retrieved from http://www.bls.gov/ooh/computer-and-information-technology/home.htm

Wai, J., Lubinski, D., & Benbow, C. (2009). Spatial ability for STEM domains: Aligning over 50 years of cumulative psychological knowledge solidifies its importance. *Journal of Educational Psychology, 101*(4), 817–835.

Wenglinsky, H. (2000). *How teaching matters: Bringing the classroom back into discussions of teacher quality* (ETS Policy Information Center Report). Princeton, NJ: Educational Testing Service. Retrieved from http://www.ets.org/research/policy_research_reports/publications/report/2000/idxn

White, R. W. (2013). Beliefs and biases in web search. In *SIGIR 2013 proceedings of the 36th international ACM SIGIR conference on research and development in information retrieval.* New York, NY: Association for Computing Machinery.

Williams, L., Kessler, R. R., Cunningham, W., & Jeffries, R. (2000). Strengthening the case for pair programming. *IEEE Software, 17*(4), 20–25. doi:10.1007/springerreference_14791

Williams, L., & Upchurch, R. L. (2001). In support of student pair-programming. *SIGCSE Bull. ACM SIGCSE Bulletin, 33*(1), 327–331. doi:10.1145/366413.364614

Wing, J. M. (2006). Computational thinking. *Communications of the ACM, 49*(3), 33. doi:10.1145/1118178.1118215

Index

CORWIN
A SAGE Publishing Company

CORWIN HAS ONE MISSION: to enhance education through intentional professional learning.

We build long-term relationships with our authors, educators, clients, and associations who partner with us to develop and continuously improve the best evidence-based practices that establish and support lifelong learning.

Solutions you want. Experts you trust. Results you need.